From our Kitchen to Yours

ALL-TIME-FAVORITE RECIPES
From

GEORGIA
COOKS

Dedication

For every cook who wants to create amazing
recipes from the great state of Georgia.

Appreciation

Thanks to all our Georgia cooks who shared their
delightful and delicious recipes with us!

Gooseberry Patch
Gooseberry Patch
An imprint of Globe Pequot
64 South Main Street
Essex, CT 06426
www.gooseberrypatch.com
1 800 854 6673

Copyright 2022, Gooseberry Patch
978-1-6209-3504-0

Do you have a tried & true recipe...tip, craft or
memory that you'd like to see featured in a
Gooseberry Patch cookbook? Visit our website at
www.gooseberrypatch.com and follow the easy steps
to submit your favorite family recipe.

Or send them to us at:

Gooseberry Patch
PO Box 812
Columbus, OH 43216-0812

Don't forget to include the number of servings your
recipe makes, plus your name, address, phone
number and email address. If we select your recipe,
your name will appear right along with it... and you'll
receive a FREE copy of the book!

GEORGIA COOKS

ICONIC GEORGIA

From the highest mountain to the swamps, rivers and ocean beaches, Georgian charm is found just about everywhere you look. In the fine state of Georgia, where music is always in the air and Christmas can be celebrated year 'round, you'll find a unique culture of friendly southern faces and delicious food that make life in Georgia peachy keen!

Established in 1732 and named after King George II of England, the state of Georgia is home to some of the most-recognized musicians in history. It is also where the history-making cotton gin was invented and the classic soda known as Coca-Cola. But despite pioneering historical inventions and cultural influences, Georgia is also a place where folks know how to slow down and take mealtime in stride.

Southern-style breakfasts are are all about taking time for a complete meal every morning, and they often include grits. Georgia has some of the finest gristmills around and so it is no surprise that grits are a staple in most Georgian kitchens and were designated as the official prepared food of Georgia. In Georgia, grits are enjoyed any time of day. They're often served as a savory meal like Shrimp & Grits for dinner, or topped with butter, a dash of cinnamon, and a sweet, juicy Georgia peach for delicious breakfast!

Inside you'll find delicious tried & true recipes from cooks from all around the great state of Georgia, including Parmesan & Cheddar Grits, Peachy-Keen Sweet Taters, Evelyn's Crab Bisque, Baked Chicken Jambalaya, Tomato-Bacon Cups, Peach Upside-Down Cake and more!

OUR STORY

Back in 1984, our families were neighbors in little Delaware, Ohio. With small children, we wanted to do what we loved and stay home with the kids too. We had always shared a love of home cooking and so, **Gooseberry Patch** was born.

Almost immediately, we found a connection with our customers and it wasn't long before these friends started sharing recipes. Since then we've enjoyed publishing hundreds of cookbooks with your tried & true recipes.

We know we couldn't have done it without our friends all across the country and we look forward to continuing to build a community with you. Welcome to the **Gooseberry Patch** family!

JoAnn & Vickie

TABLE OF CONTENTS

CHAPTER ONE

PEACHY KEEN
Breakfasts

ENJOY THESE TASTY BREAKFAST
RECIPES THAT BRING YOU TO THE
TABLE WITH A HEARTY "GOOD
MORNING!" AND CARRY YOU
THROUGH THE DAY TO TACKLE
WHATEVER COMES YOUR WAY.

MAPLE HAM & EGGS CUPS

STACI MEYERS
MONTEZUMA, GA

Ham and eggs make such a great breakfast or brunch...the kids will love the novelty too.

1 T. butter, melted
6 slices deli ham
1 T. maple syrup
1 t. butter, cut into
  6 pieces
6 eggs
salt and pepper to taste
English muffins, toast
  or biscuits

Brush muffin cups in pans with melted butter; line each cup with a slice of ham. Pour ½ teaspoon maple syrup over each ham slice; top with one pat of butter. Crack one egg into each ham cup; season with salt and pepper as desired. Bake at 400 degrees for 20 minutes, or until eggs are set. Remove muffin cups from oven; use a spoon or gently twist each serving to loosen. Serve on English muffins, with toast or on split biscuits.

Makes 6 servings.

BRANDI'S EGG & SPINACH BAKE

BRANDI TALTON
GUYTON, GA

I created this recipe for my husband. So flavorful and filling!

10 eggs, beaten
1/4 c. whipping cream
1/4 c. milk
2 t. pepper, or to taste
1/8 t. garlic salt
2 c. spinach
2 tomatoes, diced
1 c. deli ham, diced

Mix together all ingredients in a large bowl. Pour into a 12"x9" baking pan that has been sprayed with non-stick vegetable spray. Bake, uncovered, at 350 degrees for 30 minutes, or until eggs are set.

Serves 6.

MILE-HIGH BUTTERMILK BISCUITS

STACI MEYERS
MONTEZUMA, GA

The secret? Use a sharp biscuit cutter and don't twist it when cutting out your biscuits...you'll be amazed how high they rise!

Mix together flour, baking powder and salt. Cut in shortening until mixture has a crumbly texture. Stir in buttermilk until well mixed and dough leaves sides of bowl. Dough will be sticky. Knead dough 3 to 4 times on a lightly floured surface. Roll out to ½-inch thickness, about 2 to 4 passes with a rolling pin. Cut dough with a biscuit cutter, pressing straight down with cutter. Place biscuits on a parchment paper-lined baking sheet. Bake at 500 degrees for 8 to 10 minutes. Brush tops of warm biscuits with melted butter.

Makes about one dozen.

2 c. all-purpose flour
1 T. baking powder
1 t. salt
1/2 c. shortening, chilled in freezer
2/3 to 3/4 c. buttermilk
1/4 c. butter, melted

KITCHEN TIP

Use small self-adhesive hooks attached to the inside of your cabinet door for easy storage and access to small cooking utensils like measuring spoons.

CHRISTMAS MORNING RING

JULI JOHNSON
SILVER CREEK, GA

I started making this special pastry for breakfast on Christmas morning when my oldest son was a baby. Now, many years later, all three of our children look forward just as eagerly to this once-a-year-treat as they do to opening their gifts on Christmas morning!

2 8-oz. tubes refrigerated crescent rolls

12-oz. jar strawberry preserves

12-1/2 oz. can almond paste filling, thinly sliced

1 c. powdered sugar

2 t. water

1/2 t. almond extract

Spray a round pizza pan or a baking sheet with non-stick vegetable spray. Arrange crescent rolls on pan in a circle, with the points to the outside and the wide ends of the rolls overlapping each other a bit in center. Spread preserves along the center of rolls. Lay thin slices of almond paste over preserves. Fold points of rolls over almond paste; tuck under the base at center. Almond paste will not be completely covered. Bake at 375 degrees for 20 to 25 minutes, until golden. Remove from oven; let cool slightly. Meanwhile, mix remaining ingredients to make a glaze, adding more or less water for desired consistency. Drizzle glaze over crescent ring and slice.

Serves 6 to 8.

GRAB & GO BREAKFAST COOKIES

VICKIE
GOOSEBERRY PATCH

These cookies are perfect for those busy mornings when you have to rush out the door.

Blend together butter and sugar in a bowl until light and fluffy. Beat in egg, orange juice and zest; set aside. Combine flour and baking powder in a small bowl; stir into butter mixture until blended. Stir in cereal. Drop by tablespoonfuls, 2 inches apart, on an ungreased baking sheet. Bake at 350 degrees for 10 to 12 minutes, until golden around edges. Cool on a wire rack.

Makes one to 1-1/2 dozen.

1/2 c. butter, softened
1/2 c. sugar
1 egg, beaten
2 T. frozen orange juice concentrate, thawed
1 T. orange zest
1-1/4 c. all-purpose flour
1 t. baking powder
1/2 c. wheat & barley cereal

JUST FOR FUN

Georgia was named after King George II of England, who approved the colony's charter in 1732.

CREAM CHEESE MUFFINS

PAT CROWN
MARIETTA, GA

I've been making these muffins for many years for my family & friends, to go with our Christmas breakfast. They're everyone's favorite...a treat they look forward to each year! It brings me great joy to have everyone enjoying them.

1/4 c. butter, melted
1 t. vanilla extract
1/2 c. sugar
1 T. cinnamon
1/2 t. almond extract
8-oz. pkg. cream cheese
12-oz. tube refrigerated
  country-style biscuits

Combine melted butter and vanilla in a dish; mix well. In another dish, combine sugar, cinnamon and almond extract; mix well and set aside. Cut cream cheese into 10 cubes, each 1/2-inch (there may some cream cheese left over). Separate biscuits. For each muffin, dip a cream cheese cube in butter mixture; roll in sugar mixture and place in the center of a flattened biscuit. Fold biscuit over cream cheese; press seam together and roll into a ball. Dip again into butter and sugar mixtures; place seam-side down in a greased muffin cup. Repeat with remaining ingredients. Bake at 375 degrees for 15 to 18 minutes, until golden.

Makes 10 servings.

Georgia

MAPLE-PECAN BRUNCH RING

LESLIE WILLIAMS
AMERICUS, GA

A sweet & simple way to make a tasty treat for guests.

Combine pecans, brown sugar and cinnamon; set aside. Split each biscuit horizontally; brush half of the biscuits with butter and sprinkle with half the pecan mixture. Arrange topped biscuits in a circle on an ungreased baking sheet; overlap each biscuit slightly and keep within 2 inches of the edge of the baking sheet. Brush remaining biscuit halves with butter; sprinkle with remaining pecan mixture. Arrange a second ring just inside the first ring, overlapping edges. Bake at 350 degrees for 30 to 35 minutes, until golden. Remove to wire rack; cool 10 minutes. Brush with maple syrup.

Makes about 12 servings.

3/4 c. chopped pecans
1/2 c. brown sugar, packed
2 t. cinnamon
2 17.3-oz. tubes refrigerated jumbo flaky biscuits
2 T. butter, melted
1/2 c. maple syrup

JUST FOR FUN

Georgia got its nickname "The Peach State" because the Cherokee Indians grew peaches in Georgia in the mid-1700s. Today the state is the third biggest producer of peaches in the United States.

CHRISTMAS TEA

AMY BUTCHER
COLUMBUS, GA

This fruity, spiced tea is perfect for Christmas breakfasts, holiday parties or a special evening treat.

10 c. hot brewed black tea
8 c. cranberry juice
1/2 to 1 c. sugar, to taste
20 whole cloves
6 4-inch cinnamon sticks
1 lemon, thinly sliced

In a large stockpot over medium heat, simmer brewed tea, cranberry juice and sugar until sugar dissolves. Place cloves and cinnamon sticks in spice bags; add to tea along with lemon. Simmer until heated through. Serve hot or chilled.

Makes 18 servings.

LALA'S CINNAMON ROLLS

KAYLA HERRING
HARTWELL, GA

My sister found this recipe one day while scrolling the internet. The first time she made them, they were a hit! This is our family's first choice when getting together for breakfast. It pairs perfectly with coffee and your favorite breakfast casserole.

12-oz. pkg. Hawaiian sweet rolls, halved horizontally
1/2 c. butter, softened
1/4 c. brown sugar, packed
1 T. cinnamon
1/2 c. powdered sugar
2 to 3 t. milk

Arrange bottom halves of rolls in a lightly greased 13"x9" baking pan and set aside. In a small bowl, mix butter, brown sugar and cinnamon; spread half of mixture evenly over rolls. Add top halves of rolls; spread with remaining butter mixture. Bake, uncovered, at 350 degrees for 12 to 13 minutes. Stir together powdered sugar and milk; drizzle over rolls.

Makes one dozen.

DUTCH BABY WITH SPICED FRUIT

STACI PRICKETT
MONTEZUMA, GA

This is an amazing recipe...everyone loves to watch it bake! It puffs up in the oven, then slightly falls when you take it out. I often make this as a late-night treat when I want something a little sweet.

Add butter to a cast-iron skillet; place in oven at 425 degrees to melt. In a bowl, whisk together flour, sugar, salt and spice. Stir in milk, eggs and extracts; whisk until smooth. Remove hot skillet from oven; swirl butter to evenly coat bottom of skillet. Pour batter into skillet. Bake at 425 degrees for 15 to 18 minutes, until puffy and golden on edges and spots in the center. Remove from oven. Slice and serve, topped with a spoonful of Spiced Fruit and a dusting of powdered sugar.

Spiced Fruit:
Melt butter in a skillet over medium-high heat. Add apples or pears; stir until coated with butter. Cook for about 5 minutes, until fruit begins to soften. Stir together remaining ingredients; add to skillet. Cook for another 10 minutes, stirring occasionally, or until fruit is tender and sauce has thickened. Remove from heat; let cool slightly.

Makes 4 to 6 servings.

3 T. butter
1/2 c. all-purpose flour
1 T. sugar
1/4 t. salt
1/8 t. nutmeg
1/2 c. milk, room
  temperature
2 eggs, room
  temperature, beaten
1 t. vanilla extract
1/8 t. lemon extract
Garnish: powdered
  sugar

SPICED FRUIT
2 T. butter
4 apples and/or pears,
  peeled, cored and sliced
  1/4-inch thick
1/4 c. brown sugar,
  packed
1 t. cornstarch
1 t. apple pie spice
2 T. lemon juice or
  water

PARMESAN & CHEDDAR GRITS

JOANN
GOOSEBERRY PATCH

Being from Georgia, we love our grits! I serve them alongside scrambled eggs and bacon. Sometimes I'll serve this recipe at dinnertime, topped with shrimp and sweet red peppers sautéed in butter. Yum!

6 c. water
1-1/2 c. quick-cooking grits, uncooked
1 c. shredded sharp Cheddar cheese
1/2 c. shredded Parmesan cheese
2 T. half-and-half
1/2 t. salt
1/4 t. pepper

In a large saucepan, bring water to a boil. Slowly stir in grits. Reduce heat to medium-low; cover and cook until thickened, about 5 minutes, stirring occasionally. Remove from heat; stir in remaining ingredients. Cover to keep warm until serving time.

Makes 6 servings.

FAMILY-TIME CONVERSATION

Many key civil rights events were organized or enacted in Georgia. The legacy of Dr. Martin Luther King, Jr. is ever-present in Georgia where he was born, raised, preached and shaped a foundation that would lead him to becoming an icon of peace. Dr. King grew up in Atlanta in the home shared by his grandparents and parents and he lived there until he was 12. King stayed in Atlanta until he graduated from Morehouse College.

Georgia

YUMMY PEACH FREEZER JAM

CLAUDIA KELLER
CARROLLTON, GA

Summer in a jar! It isn't just for spreading on toast. Stir a spoonful into warm breakfast oatmeal...yum!

Measure exactly 3 cups chopped peaches into a large bowl. Add sugar and lemon juice; mix well. Let stand for 10 minutes, stirring occasionally. Meanwhile, combine water and pectin in a small saucepan over high heat. Bring to a boil, stirring constantly. Cook and stir for one minute; add to peach mixture. Stir for 3 minutes, until sugar is dissolved. Ladle jam into jars, leaving 1/2-inch headspace. Wipe off top edges of containers; immediately cover with lids. Let stand at room temperature for 24 hours, to allow gel to set. Refrigerate up to 3 weeks or freeze up to one year. To use, thaw overnight in refrigerator.

Makes 6, 1/2-pint jars.

2 lbs. ripe peaches, peeled, pitted and finely chopped

4-1/2 c. sugar

2 T. lemon juice

3/4 c. water

1-3/4 oz. pkg. powdered fruit pectin

6 1/2-pint plastic freezer jars and lids, sterilized

JORDAN MARSH BLUEBERRY MUFFINS

JULIE DOBSON
RICHMOND HILL, GA

When we were kids, my mom used to take my sister and me shopping at Jordan Marsh department store in Boston. We always stopped by their bakery to get a blueberry muffin. Mom got the recipe and we've made them ever since. Although the store no longer exists, we can still enjoy these wonderful muffins.

1/2 c. butter, softened
1 c. plus 2 t. sugar, divided
2 eggs
2 c. all-purpose flour
2 t. baking powder
1/2 t. salt
1/2 c. milk
1 t. vanilla extract
2-1/2 c. fresh or frozen blueberries

Combine butter and one cup sugar in a large bowl; beat with an electric mixer on medium speed until fluffy. Add eggs and beat again; set aside. In a separate bowl, sift together flour, remaining sugar, baking powder and salt. Add flour mixture to butter mixture alternately with milk and vanilla; beat until moistened. Stir in blueberries by hand. Fill greased muffin cups 2/3 full. Bake at 375 degrees for 25 to 30 minutes, until a toothpick tests clean. Cool muffins in tin for 30 minutes; remove to a wire rack.

Makes one dozen.

CATHY'S SCOTCH EGGS

JAMIE WYATT
FAYETTEVILLE, GA

My husband and I fell in love with Scotch Eggs while visiting England in 1980. Upon our return, my cousin shared her family recipe with us!

Combine sausage and herbs; mix well. Divide into 8 patties. Cover each hard-boiled egg with a sausage patty, pressing to cover and seal. Combine flour, salt and pepper. Roll eggs in flour mixture, then in beaten eggs and bread crumbs. Heat one inch of oil in a saucepan over medium-high heat. Cook eggs, a few at a time, in hot oil for 10 minutes, or until golden on all sides. Drain; chill in refrigerator. Slice into halves or quarters. Serve chilled with mustard, if desired.

Serves 8.

1 lb. ground pork sausage
2 T. dried parsley
1/2 t. dried sage
1/2 t. dried thyme
8 eggs, hard-boiled and peeled
1/2 c. all-purpose flour
1/2 t. salt
1/4 t. pepper
2 eggs, lightly beaten
1-1/2 c. dry bread crumbs
oil for frying
Optional: mustard

ZUCCHINI BREAD

DENISE WEBB
SYLVANIA, GA

I got this recipe years ago at a fruit & vegetable farm and it's the only zucchini bread I make. Moist and flavorful...it's the best! It makes two loaves, so I can share one with a friend, or freeze for later.

3 eggs, well beaten
2 c. sugar
1 c. oil
1 T. vanilla extract
2 c. zucchini, shredded
3 c. all-purpose flour
1 t. baking powder
1 t. baking soda
2 t. cinnamon
1 t. salt

In a large bowl, whisk together together eggs, sugar, oil and vanilla. Stir in zucchini; set aside. In another bowl, mix together remaining ingredients and add to zucchini mixture, stirring well. Divide batter between 2 greased and floured 9"x5" loaf pans. Bake at 350 degrees for 40 to 45 minutes, until done when tested with a toothpick. Turn loaves out of pan; cool on a wire rack.

Makes 2 loaves.

VEGGIE & SPROUTS BAGEL

JENNIFER HOLLINGSWORTH
POWDER SPRINGS, GA

I made this for myself and was amazed at how much I loved it! When my kids saw how much I liked it, they took what I had left and begged me to make more. It's such a fresh-tasting and healthy snack.

1 mini whole-wheat
bagel, halved and
lightly toasted
1 T. onion & chive
flavored cream cheese,
softened
2 T. alfalfa sprouts
2 slices tomato
2 to 4 cucumber slices
sea salt to taste

Spread each bagel half with cream cheese. Top each half with alfalfa sprouts, one tomato slice and one to 2 cucumber slices. Sprinkle with just a little salt to taste.

Makes one serving.

BETH'S EGG & CHILE BAKE

DENISE WEBB
NEWINGTON, GA

Cheesy eggs with a southwestern flair! This simple egg dish is easy to mix together and bakes in 30 minutes. Beth is a friend from church, who has often brought this dish to our breakfasts before the Sunday service. Serve with extra salsa and warm corn muffins.

Spread chiles and salsa in the bottom of a lightly greased 13"x9" baking pan. In a large bowl, whisk together eggs and cheeses; season generously with garlic salt. Spread egg mixture over salsa. Bake, uncovered, at 350 degrees for 30 minutes. Cut into squares to serve.

Makes 8 servings.

4-oz. can chopped green chiles, drained

1 c. favorite salsa, drained

1 doz. eggs, beaten

8-oz. pkg. shredded Cheddar cheese

8-oz. pkg. shredded Monterey Jack cheese

garlic salt to taste

JUST FOR FUN

Georgia hosted the Summer Olympics in 1996 in Atlanta and it is commonly referred to as the Centennial Olympic Games. These were also the last Summer Olympics to be held in North America until 2028, when Los Angeles will host the games for the third time.

MOM'S BANANA TEA BREAD

KATHY COURINGTON
CANTON, GA

Growing up, I loved the smell of this bread in the oven. My mother loved to bake and this is one of her best recipes. So yummy enjoyed warm with butter and a cup of hot tea or cocoa.

1-3/4 c. all-purpose flour
2 t. baking powder
1/4 t. baking soda
1/2 t. salt
1/3 c. shortening
2/3 c. sugar
2 eggs, lightly beaten
1 c. ripe banana, mashed

In a bowl, sift together flour, baking powder, baking soda and salt; set aside. In a separate bowl, blend together shortening and sugar; add eggs and beat well. Blend flour mixture into shortening mixture; fold in banana. Pour batter into a greased and floured 9"x5" loaf pan. Bake at 350 degrees for 50 minutes, or until a toothpick inserted in the center comes out clean. Turn loaf out of pan; cool on a wire rack.

Makes one loaf.

SUNRISE HASHBROWNS

AMY BUTCHER
COLUMBUS, GA

Absolutely the best served with eggs sunny-side-up, crispy bacon and biscuits topped with honey butter.

28-oz. pkg. frozen diced potatoes
2 c. cooked ham, cubed
2-oz. jar diced pimentos, drained
10-3/4 oz. can Cheddar cheese soup
3/4 c. milk
1/4 t. pepper

In a slow cooker, combine potatoes, ham and pimentos. In a bowl, combine soup, milk and pepper; pour over potato mixture. Cover and cook on low setting for 6 to 8 hours.

Serves 4.

QUICK AVOCADO-EGG BREAKFAST SANDWICH

CONSTANCE BOCKSTOCE
DALLAS, GA

In a hurry? This recipe takes just minutes and is easy to take along.

Toast English muffin. Meanwhile, lightly oil a 3" to 4" glass ramekin. Break egg into ramekin; break yolk with a fork. Cover with a paper towel; microwave on high for 30 to 45 seconds, until egg is completely cooked. Mash avocado onto one muffin half with a fork; carefully top avocado with cooked egg. Season with salt and pepper; top with remaining muffin half. Wrap sandwich in a napkin and serve.

Makes one sandwich.

> 1 English muffin, split
> salt and pepper to taste
> 1 egg
> 1/4 avocado, peeled, pitted and sliced

PEACHES & CREAM

CLAUDIA KELLER
CARROLLTON, GA

This is like a wonderful fruit salad, made with the most luscious ripe peaches and strawberries. We enjoy it for breakfast or as a light dessert. Can't beat our Georgia peaches!

Combine fruits in a large bowl; mix gently and set aside. In a small bowl, with an electric mixer on high speed, beat cream until it begins to thicken. Add vanilla; beat until soft peaks form. Dollop whipped cream over fruit; sprinkle with brown sugar.

Serves 4.

> 4 peaches, halved, pitted and cubed
> 1 c. strawberries, hulled and sliced
> 1 ripe banana, peeled and sliced
> 1 c. whipping cream
> 1/2 t. vanilla extract
> brown sugar to taste

BRUNCH CRESCENT CASSEROLE

BETTY KOZLOWSKI
NEWNAN, GA

I found a similar recipe online, then made a few changes to make it healthier. The first time I served it, both my grandsons went back for seconds...I think that's a pretty high recommendation!

2 8-oz. tubes refrigerated crescent rolls

1 c. baked turkey ham, cubed

6 green onions, sliced thin

5 eggs, lightly beaten

1 c. milk

1 c. fat-free half-and-half

1 t. salt

1 t. pepper

8-oz. pkg. shredded mozzarella cheese

Separate rolls; roll up each one crescent-style. Arrange rolls in 2 long rows in a greased 13"x9" baking pan. Top with ham and onions; set aside. In a bowl, whisk together remaining ingredients except cheese; fold in cheese and spoon over rolls. Bake, uncovered, at 375 degrees for 20 to 25 minutes, until golden and cheese is melted. Cut into squares.

Makes 10 servings.

SAUSAGE & CHEESE MUFFINS

JENNIFER DORWARD
JEFFERSON, GA

My mom got this recipe from a lady she used to work with. We have enjoyed it so much! We used to save these muffins for special occasions like holiday mornings, but they're just so yummy that I make them all the time now. It's great to make a big batch over the weekend, and then heat & eat on busy weekday mornings.

Brown sausage in a skillet over medium heat; drain and cool. Combine sausage with remaining ingredients; stir just until combined. Spoon mixture into greased muffin cups. Bake at 375 degrees for 15 minutes, or until golden.

Makes 12 to 16.

16-oz. pkg. ground pork breakfast sausage

10-3/4 oz. can Cheddar cheese soup

1/2 c. milk

2-1/2 c. biscuit baking mix

1 c. shredded Cheddar cheese

RED VELVET WAFFLES

AMY BUTCHER
COLUMBUS, GA

A fun and festive holiday breakfast. You'll want to use this recipe again on Valentine's Day...maybe even top with blueberries and whipped cream for the Fourth of July!

15-1/4 oz. pkg. red velvet cake mix

4 eggs, beaten

2 c. milk

Optional: 1/2 c. mini white chocolate chips

CREAM CHEESE GLAZE

1/4 c. cream cheese, softened

3 to 4 T. milk

2 c. powdered sugar

In a large bowl, combine dry cake mix, eggs and milk. Beat until smooth and well blended. Pour batter by 1/2 cupfuls into a greased, preheated waffle iron; cook according to manufacturer's instructions. Serve waffles topped with Cream Cheese Glaze. Sprinkle with mini chocolate chips, if desired.

Cream Cheese Glaze:
In a bowl, beat all ingredients with an electric mixer on medium speed until smooth.

Make 6 servings.

KITCHEN TIP

For hosting a stress-free brunch, make a brunch board. Use an oversized platter (27" or bigger) or tray and fill it with a variety of baked goods, fruits, hard-boiled eggs, cheeses and dipping bowls with jams, jellies and spreads.

APPLE BREAKFAST COBBLER

DEBI GILPIN
SHARPSBURG, GA

What a fabulous slow-cooker treat to wake up to on a chilly winter morning!

Place apples in a slow cooker sprayed with non-stick vegetable spray. In a bowl, combine remaining ingredients except garnish; sprinkle over apples. Cover and cook on low setting for 7 to 9 hours, or on high setting for 3 to 4 hours. Garnish with milk or cream.

Serves 4.

4 apples, peeled, cored and sliced
1/4 c. honey
1 t. cinnamon
2 T. butter, melted
2 c. granola cereal
Garnish: milk or cream

PECAN-RAISIN CINNAMON ROLLS

MARGARET GRAVITT
RISING FAWN, GA

I have made these cinnamon rolls for more than 25 years. We all love them! We have four children, nine grandchildren and eighteen great-grandchildren, so I often double this recipe.

4 c. all-purpose flour, divided
1 c. sugar, divided
1-1/2 oz. env. active dry yeast
1-1/2 t. salt
1-2/3 c. water
1/2 c. oil
2 eggs, beaten
1/4 c. butter, melted
1-1/2 t. cinnamon
1/2 c. raisins
1/2 c. chopped pecans
Garnish: favorite vanilla icing

POWDERED SUGAR ICING

2 c. powdered sugar
1 to 2 T. milk
1/4 c. butter, softened

In a large bowl, combine one cup flour, 1/2 cup sugar, yeast and salt; set aside. In a saucepan over medium-low heat, heat water and oil to 120 to 130 degrees; remove from heat. Add hot water mixture to flour mixture; beat just until moistened. Add eggs; beat until smooth. Stir in enough of remaining flour to form a soft, sticky dough. Turn onto floured surface; knead until smooth, about 6 to 8 minutes. Cover with a tea towel; let stand for 15 minutes. Turn dough onto a floured surface; divide in half. Roll out each half into a rectangle, 24 inches by 15 inches. Brush with melted butter to within 1/2 inch of edges. Combine remaining sugar and cinnamon; sprinkle over dough. Sprinkle with raisins and pecans. Roll up each rectangle jelly-roll style, starting on one long edge; pinch ends to seal. Cut each roll into 12 slices. Place rolls in a greased 15"x10" jelly-roll pan. Cover and let rise in a warm place until double, about 30 minutes. Bake at 425 degrees for 18 minutes, or until golden. Cool; drizzle with Powdered Sugar Icing.

Powdered Sugar Icing:
Stir together all ingredients to a drizzling consistency.

Makes 2 dozen.

MONKEY BREAD

**REBECCA IVEY
LAGRANGE, GA**

I first tried this recipe one year for a Christmas breakfast, and it was an instant hit! It's much too tasty to have just once a year.

In a saucepan over medium heat, bring butter and brown sugar to a boil. Stir until brown sugar is dissolved; cool for 10 minutes. Meanwhile, combine sugar and cinnamon in a plastic zipping bag; mix well. Add biscuit pieces, a few at a time; shake to coat well. Arrange biscuit pieces in a buttered Bundt® pan, drizzling some of brown sugar mixture over each layer. Sprinkle layers with nuts, raisins or coconut, if desired. Bake at 350 degrees for 45 minutes. Allow to cool 15 minutes before removing from pan. Turn upside-down onto a plate and serve warm.

Serves 8.

1/2 c. butter, sliced

1 c. brown sugar, packed

1 c. sugar

1-1/2 T. cinnamon

4 7-1/2 oz. tubes refrigerated biscuits, quartered

Optional: 1/2 c. raisins, chopped pecans or flaked coconut

CHAPTER TWO

ROCK CITY

Salads & Sides

TOSS TOGETHER GREAT TASTE AND
HEALTHY GOODNESS TO MAKE
FRESH, SATISFYING AND TASTY
SALADS AND SIDES THAT ARE
PACKED WITH FULL-ON FLAVOR.

BAKED OREGANO CARROTS

MELONEY EXLEY
SPRINGFIELD, GA

I have been making this for years. The oregano complements the carrots. It's a wonderful recipe for people who say they don't like carrots. May be assembled the night before and baked the next day.

1 lb. baby carrots
2 T. water
2 T. butter, sliced
1/2 t. dried oregano
1/4 t. salt

Arrange carrots in a greased 9"x9" baking pan. Add water; dot with butter. Sprinkle with seasonings. Cover and bake at 325 degrees for 1-1/4 hours, or until tender.

Makes 4 to 5 servings.

KATHY'S SAGE DRESSING

KATHY COURINGTON
CANTON, GA

I made this dressing for a Christmas party and was a little apprehensive, as I had never made dressing in a slow cooker before. I needn't have worried...everyone loved it! There was only a spoonful left.

1 onion, chopped
1/2 c. celery, chopped
6 T. butter, divided
12-oz. pkg. cornbread stuffing
12-oz. pkg. herb-seasoned stuffing
4 eggs, lightly beaten
2 T. dried sage
1 t. salt
1/2 t. pepper
2 10-3/4 oz. cans cream of chicken soup
2 to 4 14-oz. cans chicken broth

In a skillet over medium heat, sauté onion and celery in 2 tablespoons butter for about 5 minutes. In a large bowl, combine cornbread stuffing, seasoned stuffing, onion mixture, eggs, seasonings and soup; mix well. Add 2 cans broth and mix well. Additional broth may be added, depending on moistness desired. Spoon into a greased 6-quart slow cooker; dot with remaining butter. Cover and cook on high setting for 2 hours, or on low setting for 4 hours. If mixture becomes too dry, add more broth or water.

Serves 12 to 16.

GRANDMA'S SLOPPY KRAUT

LINDA NAGY
POWDER SPRINGS, GA

Growing up in a German household meant that sauerkraut was a staple and a great side dish, paired with sausage or pork and potatoes. New Year's Day was always celebrated with pork roast and Grandma's specialty...her hearty Sloppy Kraut, a German tradition for good luck throughout the year.

Cook bacon in a large skillet over medium heat until almost crisp. Leave bacon and drippings in pan. Add remaining ingredients except water and pepper; stir to combine. Cook over medium heat, adding water a little at a time, until heated through. Cover and simmer over low heat for 15 minutes, stirring occasionally. Season with pepper and serve.

Makes 4 to 6 servings.

4 slices bacon, cut into 1-1/2 inch pieces

14.4-oz. can sauerkraut, drained

1/2 c. onion, grated

1 small potato, grated

1 small apple, peeled, cored and grated

1-1/2 t. caraway seed

1/2 c. water

pepper to taste

PATTERSONS' POTATO CASSEROLE

JOALICE PATTERSON–WELTON
LAWRENCEVILLE, GA

This is such an easy and delicious side dish. My mom, who was a wonderful southern cook, used to make this in the fall and winter whenever she baked a beef tenderloin.

Layer potato and onion slices in a greased 3-quart casserole dish; set aside. In a bowl, mix together remaining ingredients; spoon over top. Bake, uncovered, at 375 degrees for one hour, or until potatoes are tender and golden.

Makes 4 to 6 servings.

4 to 6 baking potatoes, peeled and sliced

1 onion, sliced

10-3/4 oz. can cream of chicken soup

1/2 c. milk

1/4 c. butter, melted

salt and pepper to taste

ALMOND GREEN BEANS WITH MUSHROOMS

KATHY COURINGTON
CANTON, GA

My husband likes green beans, and he loves these with the crunch of almonds. Easy for everyday, yet good enough for company!

1/2 c. shallots or onion, chopped
1-1/2 c. sliced mushrooms
1/4 c. slivered almonds, divided
10-3/4 oz. can cream of mushroom soup
2 14-1/2 oz. cans cut green beans, drained
1/4 t. pepper

Spray a large skillet with non-stick vegetable spray. Add shallots or onion; sauté over medium heat for 5 minutes, or until tender. Add mushrooms and half of almonds; stir. Cook for 2 to 3 minutes. Stir in mushroom soup, green beans and pepper. Reduce heat to medium-low and simmer for 5 minutes, stirring occasionally, or until mixture is heated through. Top with remaining almonds and serve.

Serves 4.

SWEET POTATO FRIES

TINA WRIGHT
ATLANTA, GA

A tasty side for burgers and sandwiches! If you like them sweet, add 2 tablespoons brown sugar and 1/2 teaspoon cinnamon along with the oil and salt.

4 sweet potatoes, peeled and cut into strips
1 T. olive oil
1 t. salt

Place sweet potato strips in a large bowl. Add oil and salt; toss well to coat. Arrange on a lightly greased baking sheet. Bake on center rack of oven at 425 degrees for 20 minutes. Turn over; bake another 15 minutes, or until tender. Serve immediately.

Serves 4.

MOM'S DIRTY RICE

BETTY KOZLOWSKI
NEWNAN, GA

*We had a large family, and all of us loved Mom's Dirty Rice! Whenever
we visited Grandma's for a butchering, this Cajun-style rice dressing was
always on the menu, along with cracklings made using the fresh pork.*

In a food processor, grind chicken livers and
gizzards; set aside. Add livers, gizzards and oil to a
large skillet over medium heat; cook until browned.
Drain, leaving livers and gizzards in pan. To the
same pan, add butter, pork, onions and green
pepper. Sauté for 5 minutes. Add one cup water;
cover and simmer for 5 minutes. Uncover and cook
until liquid is absorbed. Add salt and remaining
water. Bring to a boil over high heat. Stir in uncooked
rice and pepper; bring to a boil again. Reduce heat
to medium-low; cover and simmer for 15 minutes.
Gently fold rice mixture from top to bottom with a
large spoon. Cover and cook for about 5 to
10 minutes, until rice is tender and water is
absorbed. Garnish as desired and serve.

Makes 8 servings.

1 lb. chicken livers
1 lb. chicken gizzards
1 T. oil
1 T. butter
1 lb. ground pork
2 onions, chopped
1 green pepper, chopped
5 c. water, divided
2 to 3 t. salt
2 c. long-grain rice,
  uncooked
1 t. pepper
Garnish: chopped green
  onion, fresh parsley

PRESENTATION

Simple garnishes dress up main dishes
all year 'round! Fresh mint sprigs
add coolness and color to summertime
dishes, while rosemary sprigs and
cranberries add a festive touch to
holiday platters.

LAYERED CARIBBEAN CHICKEN SALAD

LAUREL PERRY
LOGANVILLE, GA

This is a wonderful way to use rotisserie chicken from the deli. You won't believe how yummy the dressing is!

3 c. romaine lettuce, shredded

2 c. cooked chicken, cubed

1 c. shredded Monterey Jack cheese

15-1/2 oz. can black beans, drained and rinsed

1-1/2 c. mango, halved, pitted and cubed

1/2 c. plum tomatoes, chopped

1 c. shredded Cheddar cheese

1/2 c. green onions, thinly sliced

1/2 c. cashews, chopped

In a large clear glass serving bowl, layer all salad ingredients in order listed, except cashews. Spoon Dressing evenly over salad; sprinkle cashews over top.

Dressing:
In a small bowl, mix all ingredients together until well blended.

Makes 6 servings.

DRESSING

6-oz. container piña colada yogurt

2 T. lime juice

1 t. Caribbean jerk seasoning

A LITTLE DIFFERENT MACARONI SALAD

WANDA WILSON
HAMILTON, GA

Sweetened condensed milk is the secret ingredient!

Combine macaroni, carrots, onion and peppers in a large bowl. In a separate bowl, whisk together mayonnaise, condensed milk, sugar and vinegar. Pour over macaroni and vegetables. Season with salt and pepper. Chill at least 8 hours to allow dressing to thicken. Mix well before serving.

Makes 8 to 10 servings.

16-oz. pkg. elbow macaroni, cooked

4 carrots, peeled and grated

1 sweet onion, chopped

1/2 c. red pepper, chopped

1/2 c. green pepper, chopped

2 c. mayonnaise

14-oz. can sweetened condensed milk

1/4 to 1/2 c. sugar

1/2 c. white vinegar

salt and pepper to taste

CRANBERRY PRETZEL SALAD

RONDA SIERRA
WOODSTOCK, GA

Our Thanksgiving meal would not be complete without this yummy side dish...or is it a dessert? Whatever you call it, it's scrumptious!

2 c. boiling water

6-oz. pkg. black cherry gelatin mix

2 15-oz. cans whole-berry cranberry sauce

2 c. pretzel twists, finely crushed

3/4 c. butter, melted

1/2 c. plus 1 T. sugar, divided

8-oz. pkg. cream cheese, softened

8-oz. container frozen whipped topping, thawed

In a bowl, stir together boiling water and gelatin mix for 2 minutes, or until dissolved. Stir in cranberry sauce. Cover and refrigerate until cooled and partially set. Meanwhile, in a separate bowl, mix together crushed pretzels, melted butter and one tablespoon sugar. Press into the bottom of an ungreased 13"x9" glass baking pan. Bake at 350 degrees for 8 minutes; set aside to cool. In another bowl, blend together cream cheese, whipped topping and remaining sugar; spread over cooled crust. Spoon cooled gelatin over cream cheese mixture. Cover and refrigerate overnight, or until set. Cut into squares.

Serves 12.

DINNERTIME CONVERSATION

Georgia has more soil types than any other state: loam, silt and clay, and it grows the most peanuts and pecans. The 39th President, Jimmy Carter, was a peanut farmer from Georgia.

BROCCOLI CASSEROLE

KATHY COURINGTON
CANTON, GA

I first sampled this dish at church potluck and have loved it ever since. Easy and delicious.

In a large bowl, mix together broccoli, soup, cheese, mayonnaise and eggs. Transfer to a lightly greased 2-quart casserole dish. Mix crushed crackers with melted butter; spread over casserole. Bake, uncovered, at 350 degrees for 30 minutes, or until hot and bubbly.

Serves 4 to 6.

- 2 10-oz. pkg's. frozen chopped broccoli, thawed and drained
- 10-3/4 oz. can cream of mushroom soup
- 1 c. shredded Cheddar cheese
- 1 c. mayonnaise
- 2 eggs, beaten
- 1 c. cheese crackers, crushed
- 1 T. butter, melted

UPDATED GREEN BEAN CASSEROLE

TINA WRIGHT
ATLANTA, GA

My husband can't stand mushroom soup, but he loves those crispy onions, so I was happy when I found this recipe. We love it!

Place beans in a microwave-safe 2-quart casserole dish; cover and microwave for 10 minutes. Meanwhile, melt butter in a saucepan over medium heat. Sprinkle with flour; cook and stir for one minute, or until lightly golden. Add broth; cook, whisking constantly, until thickened and smooth. Whisk in milk; cook until thickened. Stir in all the onions. Spoon over beans in dish. Bake, uncovered, at 350 degrees for 30 minutes.

Serves 8 to 10.

- 16-oz. pkg. frozen French-cut green beans
- 2 T. butter
- 1/4 c. all-purpose flour
- 1 c. chicken broth
- 1 c. whole milk
- 1 c. canned French fried onions
- 1 T. dried, minced onion

TOMATO FRITTERS

DEANNE CORONA
HAMPTON, GA

*I have no idea where my grandmother picked up this gem of a recipe...
she was using it as a bookmark in one of her cookbooks. The first time
I tried it, I fell in love. It's really good with chicken or any other main
dish. I love tomatoes and can eat them off the vine just as they are,
but sometimes they just need that extra oomph. So here is one of my
favorite sides using fresh tomatoes!*

1 c. all-purpose flour
1 t. baking powder
1 t. fresh rosemary,
  snipped
1/8 t. salt
1/8 t. pepper
1 c. ripe tomatoes, cut
  into 1/2-inch cubes
2 T. onion or leek, finely
  chopped
1 T. fresh basil, snipped
1/8 t. Worcestershire
  sauce
1 egg, beaten
oil for frying
Optional: cheese or
  jalapeño jelly

In a bowl, combine flour, baking powder, rosemary, salt and pepper. Pat tomatoes dry; add to flour mixture. Add remaining ingredients except egg, oil and optional ingredients; don't mix yet. Add egg and stir everything together. In a large skillet over medium-high heat, heat several inches oil to at least 360 degrees. Drop batter into oil by tablespoonfuls, lightly patting them down a bit into the hot oil. Cook until golden on both sides; drain on paper towels. Serve with cheese or jalapeño jelly, if desired.

Serves 4 to 6.

BLITZBURGH BEANS

STACI PRICKETT
MONTEZUMA, GA

A favorite tailgating side of ours...give it a try, and it's sure to become yours too!

In a large skillet over medium heat, brown together beef, sausage and bacon; drain. Add onion and green pepper; cook until slightly tender. Stir in brown sugar, catsup, salt and pepper. Add all beans; do not drain cans. Mix well. Transfer to a greased 13"x9" baking pan. Bake, uncovered, at 350 degrees for 40 to 50 minutes, until hot and bubbly.

Makes 8 to 12 servings.

1/2 lb. ground beef

1/2 lb. Kielbasa sausage, sliced into 1-inch pieces

1/2 lb. bacon, sliced into 1-inch pieces

1/2 c. onion, chopped

1/2 c. green pepper, chopped

3/4 c. brown sugar, packed

1/2 c. catsup

salt and pepper to taste

2 16-oz. cans pork & beans

2 15-1/2 oz. cans kidney beans

2 15-1/2 oz. cans butter beans

KITCHEN TIP

A dollop of lemon butter adds flavor to plain steamed vegetables. Simply blend 2 tablespoons softened butter with the zest of one lemon.

GEORGIA GREEN BEANS & POTATOES

TINA WRIGHT
ATLANTA, GA

My aunt always said there was nothing better than a mess of fresh green beans! They're a meal in themselves with a pan of cornbread.

6 slices bacon, cut into
  1-inch pieces and
  partially cooked
4 to 6 redskin potatoes,
  thinly sliced
4 to 5 c. green beans,
  trimmed
10-3/4 oz. can cream of
  celery soup
2 T. dried, minced onion
salt and pepper to taste

Combine all ingredients in a large slow cooker; stir gently. Cover and cook on low setting for 7 to 9 hours.

Serves 4 to 6.

HEARTY RED BEANS & RICE

**LAUREL PERRY
LOGANVILLE, GA**

A delicious recipe that makes enough to feed a crowd. Pass the hot sauce, please!

Cover beans with water; soak for 6 to 8 hours. Drain; rinse well and set aside. Cook bacon in a Dutch oven over medium-high heat for 5 minutes. Add Kielbasa and ham; cook until browned. Add garlic and vegetables; cook until tender. Stir in beans, chicken broth, water and seasonings. Bring to a boil. Reduce heat to low. Simmer, stirring occasionally, for 3 hours, or until beans are tender. Serve over cooked rice.

Makes 12 servings.

2 lbs. dried red kidney beans

7 slices bacon, coarsely chopped into chunks

2 lbs. Kielbasa sausage, sliced 1/4-inch thick on the diagonal

1-1/2 c. cooked ham, diced

6 cloves garlic, minced

4 stalks celery, diced

2 green peppers, diced

2 onions, chopped

8 c. chicken broth

2 c. water

1/8 to 1/4 t. seafood seasoning

salt and pepper to taste

cooked rice

GINA'S SOUTHERN GREEN BEANS

GINA MCCLENNING
NICHOLSON, GA

These tender green beans are absolutely delicious as a side with chicken or pork.

2 slices bacon
2 large slices onion, chopped
2 T. oil
1 clove garlic, minced
salt and pepper to taste
1 to 2 drops hot pepper sauce
red wine vinegar or balsamic vinegar to taste
1 lb. fresh green beans, trimmed and snapped

In a large saucepan over medium heat, cook bacon with onion for 3 minutes. Stir in oil, garlic, seasonings, hot sauce and a splash of vinegar. Add beans; stir to coat. Reduce heat to medium-low. Cover and cook for 5 minutes; stir. Reduce heat to low. Cook for about 25 minutes, or until beans are tender and coated with a brown sauce.

Makes 4 servings.

HEAVENLY POTATOES

CAMILLE JONES
SUWANEE, GA

Easy to make and SO scrumptious!

1 onion, finely chopped
2 T. butter
24-oz. pkg. frozen shredded hashbrowns, thawed
2 c. shredded sharp Cheddar cheese
10-3/4 oz. can cream of chicken soup
2 c. sour cream
salt and pepper to taste

Sauté onion in butter until tender; combine with remaining ingredients. Pour into a 2-quart casserole dish. Bake at 350 degrees for one hour.

Makes 8 to 10 servings.

SOUTHERN CORNBREAD SALAD

STACI PRICKETT
MONTEZUMA, GA

A sweet twist on a layered salad! This recipe is a huge hit at potlucks and socials. The sweet cornbread and tangy buttermilk ranch complement each other so well...the bowl is always empty and the recipe is requested.

Prepare and bake corn muffin mix according to package instructions, using an 8"x8" baking pan. Set aside to cool completely. In a bowl, mix together mayonnaise, sour cream and salad dressing mix; cover and chill. To assemble, crumble half of cornbread into a clear glass trifle bowl. Top with half of each vegetable, either layered separately or mixed together. Spread half of mayonnaise mixture over vegetables; top with one cup of cheese and half of the bacon bits. Repeat layers, ending with bacon bits. Cover and refrigerate overnight; serve cold.

Makes 8 to 10 servings.

- 8-1/2 oz. pkg. corn muffin mix
- 1 c. mayonnaise
- 1 c. sour cream
- 4-oz. pkg. buttermilk ranch salad dressing mix
- 1/2 c. red or sweet onion, diced
- 1/2 c. green or red pepper, diced
- 2 to 3 tomatoes, diced
- 15-oz. can corn, drained
- 15-oz. can peas, drained
- 8-oz. pkg. shredded sharp Cheddar cheese, divided
- 3-oz. pkg. real bacon bits, divided

CHEESY BACON CASSEROLE

LAURA STRAUSBERGER
ROSWELL, GA

Just the right size casserole for a small family. Double the recipe if you want to feed more.

4 slices white bread, crusts trimmed
4 eggs, beaten
1-1/2 c. milk
1 t. dry mustard
1/2 t. dried, chopped onion
8 slices bacon, crisply cooked and crumbled
1 c. shredded Cheddar cheese

Arrange bread slices in a lightly greased 8"x8" baking pan; set aside. Stir together eggs, milk, mustard and onion; pour over bread. Sprinkle with bacon; cover and refrigerate 8 hours or overnight. Let stand at room temperature for 30 minutes; uncover and bake at 350 degrees for 20 minutes. Sprinkle with cheese and bake an additional 5 minutes, until cheese melts.

Makes 4 servings.

DINNERTIME CONVERSATION

While the oddly well-known roadside attraction of Rock City is often associated with Chattanooga, Tennessee, it is actually located in Lookout Mountain, Georgia. This park blends a beautiful natural setting atop Lookout Mountain with a variety of garden gnomes hidden throughout the landscape. You can gaze at a 100-foot waterfall, cross a 200-foot long swinging bridge, and edge your way through the narrow rock passageway known as "Fat Man's Squeeze."

AUNT RUBY'S SPINACH CASSEROLE

JOALICE PATTERSON–WELTON
LAWRENCEVILLE, GA

This is a family hand-me-down-recipe from my aunt, who passed away many years ago. She loved making this for the family and we loved to eat it. Wonderful with chicken and beef dishes.

Cook spinach according to package directions. Drain well, using a paper towel to blot out excess water. Transfer to a lightly greased 2-quart casserole dish. Add butter, sour cream, soup mix and stuffing crumbs. Mix together well to blend. Bake, uncovered, at 350 degrees for 20 minutes, or until heated through.

Serves 4 to 6.

2 10-oz. pkgs. frozen chopped spinach

1/2 c. butter, sliced

8-oz. container sour cream

1.35-oz. pkg. onion soup mix

2 c. herb-seasoned stuffing

CREAMY SCALLOPED POTATOES

DELINDA BLAKNEY
DALLAS, GA

Who can resist scalloped potatoes? They go with practically any main dish!

Mix soup, milk, parsley, salt and pepper together; set aside. Layer half the potatoes in a buttered 1-1/2 quart casserole dish; top with 1/2 cup onion. Repeat layers; spread soup mixture on top. Cover; bake at 350 degrees until potatoes are soft, about one hour.

Serves 4.

10-3/4 oz. can cream of chicken soup

1/2 c. milk

1/4 c. fresh parsley, minced

1 t. salt

1 t. pepper

4 c. potatoes, peeled, sliced and divided

1 onion, chopped and divided

PEACHY-KEEN SWEET TATERS

**CATHI CARPENTER
MARIETTA, GA**

I make these sweet potatoes for every holiday...it's the only way our eight-year-old son will eat them! Try this dish with apple pie filling too, substituting apple pie spice for the ginger. Yummy!

2-1/4 c. sweet potatoes, peeled and cubed

21-oz. can peach pie filling

2 T. butter, melted

1 t. fresh ginger, peeled and grated, or 1 t. ground ginger

1/4 t. salt

2 T. brown sugar, packed

1/8 t. cinnamon

1/2 c. pecans, coarsely chopped

Place sweet potatoes in a 4-quart slow cooker sprayed with non-stick vegetable spray. Add pie filling, butter, ginger and salt; mix well to coat. Cover and cook on high setting for 2-1/2 to 3 hours. In a small saucepan over medium-low heat, combine remaining ingredients. Cook until glazed and bubbly, stirring frequently. Spoon pecans onto an aluminum foil-lined baking sheet to cool. Just before serving, gently stir potatoes; sprinkle with pecans.

Serves 6.

KITCHEN TIP

To dress up your drinks, place berries or edible flowers into an ice-cube tray with water and freeze. Once frozen, pop the cubes into a pretty glass.

CORN & BACON SAUTÉ

KIM MCCALLIE
GUYTON, GA

I created this recipe to use up some ingredients I had in the refrigerator. It was so good that I'm making sure I keep the ingredients on hand so that I can enjoy it more often.

Heat oil in a large skillet over medium-low heat. Sauté bacon and onion until bacon starts to get crisp, about 10 minutes. Remove bacon mixture with a slotted spoon and set aside, reserving drippings. Add corn and seasonings to drippings in skillet. Increase heat to medium-high; cook until corn is heated through and any moisture is cooked out. Return bacon mixture to the skillet; mix together well. Remove from heat; stir in green onions.

Serves 4 to 6.

1 t. olive oil

6 slices bacon, diced

1/2 onion, chopped

16-oz. pkg. frozen corn

kosher salt and coarse pepper to taste

dried thyme to taste

4 to 5 green onions, sliced

ALICE'S BROWN SUGARED APRICOTS

JOALICE PATTERSON–WELTON
LAWRENCEVILLE, GA

A family favorite! This is a recipe my late mother conjured up in the kitchen one day as she was looking for a different kind of side dish for the baked chicken dinner she was cooking. I am blessed that my mom was a wonderful Southern cook.

Arrange apricots in a lightly greased 13"x9" baking pan. Combine crushed crackers with brown sugar; crumble over apricots. Drizzle with melted butter. Bake, uncovered, at 300 degrees for 40 minutes. Serve warm.

Makes 6 to 8 servings.

3 17-oz. cans sliced apricots, drained

1 c. light brown sugar, packed

1/2 c. butter, melted

1 sleeve round buttery crackers, crushed

ENGLISH PEA CASSEROLE

KATHY BARRY
BONAIRE, GA

This is a family favorite, and is also highly requested for luncheons at work. Sometimes I don't make it to the sign-up sheet fast enough...but somebody has already written down my name for this recipe! Easy to make, and a perfect side dish for all occasions.

3 to 4 15-oz. cans young sweet peas, drained

10-3/4 oz. can cream of mushroom soup

8-oz. container sour cream

1 t. garlic powder

1 c. shredded Cheddar cheese

1-1/2 sleeves round buttery crackers, crushed

3/4 c. margarine, melted

Add peas to a bowl; set aside. In another bowl, mix mushroom soup, sour cream and garlic powder. Fold into peas; transfer to a lightly greased 3-quart casserole dish. Top with shredded cheese and crushed crackers. Drizzle melted margarine over crackers. Bake, uncovered, at 350 degrees for 45 minutes to one hour, until hot and bubbly.

Makes 6 to 8 servings.

NEIGHBOR RUTH'S SLAW

JUDY COLLINS
ROSWELL, GA

This salad uses sweet Vidalia onions from here in Georgia.

1 cabbage, shredded

1 yellow crookneck squash, sliced thinly and diced

1 red or green pepper, chopped

1 sweet onion, chopped

1/2 c. sugar

1/2 c. vinegar

1/2 c. oil

1 T. salt

Layer all vegetables in a serving bowl; sprinkle with sugar and set aside. In a small saucepan over low heat, bring vinegar, oil and salt to a boil; mix well. Pour over cabbage; do not stir. Cover and refrigerate at least 4 hours to overnight. Stir to serve. May be kept refrigerated for a week.

Makes 8 servings.

ISRAELI SALAD

CAROL LOWERY
EASTMAN, GA

This recipe was given to me by friends from Colorado while they were staying at our horse farm. If you'd like, add olives, chickpeas, jalapeños and diced avocados. It can even be spooned into a pita pocket for easy serving.

Combine all ingredients in a large bowl; mix well. Serve immediately, or cover and chill.

Makes 6 to 8 servings.

2 to 4 cucumbers, diced
4 tomatoes, diced
1 green pepper, diced
1 red pepper, diced
1 onion, diced
2 c. canned corn
2 T. olive oil
1 t. salt
1 T. lemon juice

EGG DROP RAMEN

LAURA SEBAN
SAINT SIMONS ISLAND, GA

This is a true penny-pinching recipe that I created myself. I can fix it for under a dollar with ingredients I have on hand. My daughter loves it...and so do most other people when they give it a try!

In a saucepan, bring water to a boil over medium heat. Add half of the seasoning packet, reserving the rest for another use. Stir in noodles; cook for 3 minutes. Add eggs, stirring quickly for 2 minutes to break them up. Add cheese and stir in well. Remove from heat; mix in peas. Serve in soup bowls.

Makes 2 to 3 servings.

1-1/2 c. water
3-oz. pkg. chicken-flavored ramen noodles, uncooked and divided
2 eggs, beaten
2 slices American cheese, chopped
1/3 c. peas

Georgia

CHAPTER THREE

SOUL MUSIC

Soups & Sandwiches

GATHER 'ROUND THE TABLE

TOGETHER WITH FAMILY & FRIENDS

OR COZY UP WITH A BOWL

OF HEARTY SOUP OR A TASTY

SANDWICH PERFECT, FOR AN

AFTERNOON ON THE FRONT PORCH

IN YOUR FAVORITE ROCKING CHAIR.

MEATBALLS & VEGGIES CHEESE SOUP

DENISE WEBB
GUYTON, GA

This is such a great comforting soup on all those busy, cold days of winter. Serve with a hearty country-style bread.

1 lb. ground beef
1/4 c. soft bread crumbs
1 egg, beaten
1/2 t. hot pepper sauce
1/2 t. salt
2 c. water
1 c. celery, chopped
1/2 c. onion, chopped
2 cubes beef bouillon
1 c. canned or frozen corn
1 c. potatoes, peeled and sliced
1/2 c. carrots, peeled and sliced
16-oz. jar pasteurized process cheese dip

In a bowl, mix together beef, bread crumbs, egg, hot sauce and salt. Roll into small balls; place in a 5-quart slow cooker. Add remaining ingredients except cheese. Cover and cook on low setting for 8 to 10 hours. Just before serving, stir in cheese.

Serves 6 to 8.

CHICKEN CORN SOUP

SANDI TOWNSEND
PLAINVILLE, GA

This is a wonderful creamy soup that I've been making for years.
I usually triple the recipe so I'll have some left over to freeze.

Melt chicken fat or margarine in a skillet over medium heat; sauté onion and carrot until tender. Sprinkle with flour and simmer for 5 minutes. Add chicken broth; stir well. Add corn, half-and-half or milk, pepper and parsley; stir well and simmer for 3 to 4 minutes. Stir in chicken; simmer until heated through.

Serves 8 to 10.

6 T. chicken fat or margarine

1/2 c. onion, diced

2 T. carrot, peeled and grated

6 T. all-purpose flour

2 c. chicken broth

14-3/4 oz. can creamed corn

1-1/2 c. half-and-half or whole milk

1/4 t. pepper

chopped fresh parsley to taste

1-1/2 c. cooked chicken, diced

DINNERTIME CONVERSATION

Georgia's musical history is vast and diverse across many genres and had historical impacts on african-american folk music, country, jazz, blues, hip hop and rock music. The African-American musical and dance tradition "ring shout" is rare to find in the modern United States, but can still be found in McIntosh County in Georgia.

EVELYN'S CRAB BISQUE

**TINA WRIGHT
ATLANTA, GA**

My grandmother who lived in Maryland loved to make crab dishes for special family occasions. Sometimes she saved out a little of the crabmeat and parsley to use as a garnish.

6 T. butter, divided

1/4 c. green pepper, diced

1/4 c. white onion, diced

1 green onion, diced

2 T. fresh parsley, snipped

2 T. all-purpose flour

1-1/2 c. half-and-half

1 c. whole milk

salt to taste

1 t. pepper

6-oz. can crabmeat, drained and flaked

Melt 4 tablespoons butter in a skillet over medium-high heat. Add vegetables and parsley; sauté for 5 minutes. Meanwhile, melt remaining butter in a saucepan over medium heat. Sprinkle with flour; stir until well blended. Add half-and-half and milk; cook and stir until thickened. Stir in salt and pepper. Reduce heat to low; stir in crabmeat and simmer for 5 minutes.

Makes 4 servings.

JUST FOR FUN

The song "Georgia on My Mind" was written about the state of Georgia in 1930 by Hoagy Carmichael and Stuart Gorrell and first recorded by Carmichael. Thirty years later it became a number one pop-hit after it was rerecorded by Ray Charles.

EASY TACO SOUP

KATHY COURINGTON
CANTON, GA

I made this slow-cooker soup for a church workday and everyone loved it, so I kept the recipe. Great for potlucks, as it makes a crockful of goodness. Very yummy and satisfying! Serve with tortilla chips or cornbread muffins.

In a 6-quart slow cooker, combine all ingredients except garnish. Do not drain tomatoes or beans. Cover and cook on low setting for 6 to 8 hours. Serve topped with shredded cheese and sour cream.

Makes 8 to 10 servings.

2 lbs. ground beef, browned and drained
1 onion, diced
4 14-1/2 oz. cans diced tomatoes
15-oz. kidney beans
15-oz. pinto beans
15-1/4 oz. sweet corn & diced peppers, drained
4-oz. can diced green chiles, drained
1-oz. pkg. taco seasoning mix
1-oz. pkg. ranch salad dressing mix
Garnish: shredded cheese, sour cream

CREAMY WILD RICE CHICKEN SOUP

BETTY KOZLOWSKI
NEWNAN, GA

We love soups at our house, no matter the season! This slow-cooker recipe has become a family favorite. Very comforting on a chilly day.

5 c. water
6-oz. pkg. chicken-flavored long-grain & wild rice mix
10-3/4 oz. can cream of mushroom soup
4-oz. can sliced mushrooms, drained
1/2 t. dried thyme
1/4 t. pepper
1 c. cooked chicken, cubed
10-oz. pkg. frozen chopped spinach or kale, thawed

In a 5-quart slow cooker, combine all ingredients except chicken and spinach or kale; stir. Cover and cook on low setting for 7 to 8 hours, or on high setting for 3-1/2 to 4 hours. Stir in chicken and spinach or kale. Cover and continue cooking until heated through, 10 to 20 minutes.

Variation: For a heartier soup with a richer broth, use 2 to 4 pieces of uncooked bone-in chicken, adding it at the beginning. Cook as directed. Remove chicken when cooked through. Stir in spinach as directed; chop or shred chicken and return to soup.

Makes 6 servings.

DINNERTIME CONVERSATION

Georgia has hundreds of radio stations and several dozen television stations. Cable News Network (CNN), the first cable television channel to offer continuous broadcasting, was established in Atlanta in 1980 and later became one of the leaders in domestic and international television journalism.

Georgia

CONSTANCE'S CABBAGE SOUP

CONSTANCE BOCKSTOCE
DALLAS, GA

Ever since I was a young child...over 60 years ago!...I have eaten this soup for dinner on cold evenings. It has been a favorite for my children and my grandchildren. Tastes great the next day, too.

Layer ingredients in a large stockpot in the order listed. Bring to a boil over medium-high heat. Turn down heat to medium-low. Cover and simmer for one hour, or until vegetables are tender, stirring occasionally.

Makes 6 to 8 servings.

32-oz. container chicken broth

1/2 to 1 head cabbage, cut into large cubes

2 lbs. baby carrots, cut in half

1 lb. smoked pork sausage link, sliced 1/2-inch thick

2 lbs. potatoes, peeled and cut into large cubes

2 T. onion, finely chopped

1 t. pepper, or to taste

Optional: 1 t. dried basil

BUFFALO CHICKEN WRAPS

VICKIE
GOOSEBERRY PATCH

My family loves chicken wings! These wraps have all their favorite flavors...great for casual meals when the kids bring home a friend or two for dinner. Just add a chopped salad and some chips.

1/2 to 1 lb. bacon

1-1/2 lbs. boneless chicken tenderloins

1 c. buffalo wing sauce, divided

8 10-inch flour tortillas, warmed

8 lettuce leaves

1 green pepper, cut into strips

1/2 c. ranch salad dressing

Optional: additional ranch dressing, celery sticks

In a large skillet over medium heat, cook bacon until crisp; set aside to drain on paper towels. Meanwhile, add chicken tenderloins and 1/2 cup sauce to another skillet over medium heat. Bring to a boil; reduce heat to medium-low. Cook for 10 to 12 minutes, stirring occasionally, until chicken juices run clear when pierced. Remove chicken from heat; cool slightly, then shred with 2 forks. To serve, top each tortilla with a lettuce leaf; spoon 1/2 cup chicken mixture down the center. Top with bacon and green pepper. Drizzle with salad dressing and remaining sauce; roll up. Garnish as desired.

Makes 8 servings.

MEATBALL & TORTELLINI SOUP

KATHY COURINGTON
CANTON, GA

I had never fixed meatballs this way and wanted to try something different. My husband said this slow-cooker recipe was a keeper! Very warming-to-the-tummy goodness.

Place frozen meatballs in a 5-quart slow cooker. Add tomatoes with juice, broth, onion, seasoning and garlic. Cover and cook on low setting for 6 hours, or on high setting for 4 hours. During the last hour, add tortellini to slow cooker. Serve topped with cheeses.

Makes 4 to 6 servings.

25-oz. pkg. frozen
    meatballs
2 14-1/2 oz. cans stewed
    tomatoes
32-oz. container beef or
    vegetable broth
1 onion, chopped
2 T. Italian seasoning
2 t. garlic, minced
16-oz. pkg. refrigerated
    cheese tortellini,
    uncooked
Garnish: shredded
    Parmesan and
    mozzarella cheeses

PRESENTATION

Dress up sandwiches by individually wrapping them in brown parchment paper. Seal the paper with a sticker that matches the theme of your party.

AMY'S HARVEST CHILI

AMY SOLEN
TENNILLE, GA

My family loves this slow-cooker recipe when the weather starts to change. It warms us right up. Add a basket of cornbread...yum!

1 lb. ground beef
15-1/2 oz. can light red kidney beans
15-1/2 oz. can dark red kidney beans
15-1/2 oz. can Great Northern beans
15-1/2 oz. can pinto beans
15-1/2 oz. can red beans
15-1/2 oz. can chili beans
2 1-1/4 oz. pkg's. mild chili seasoning mix
Garnish: shredded Cheddar cheese, sour cream

Brown beef in a skillet over medium heat; drain. Add all the cans of beans with their juices to a 5-quart slow cooker. Stir in beef and chili seasoning. Cover and cook on low setting for 6 to 8 hours. Garnish as desired.

Serves 8.

YUMMY EASY CORN CHOWDER

KATHY COURINGTON
CANTON, GA

The first time I tasted this soup, I thought, "Wow, is this good!" Our pastor's wife said at the time that it was easy to make too. She was kind enough to give me the recipe.

In a large skillet over medium heat, cook sausage and onion until sausage is browned; drain. Stir in milks and water; bring to a boil. Add both cans of corn, potato and seasonings. Reduce heat to medium-low and simmer for 1-1/2 to 2 hours, stirring occasionally. If too thick, stir in a little more milk or water.

Makes 6 to 8 servings.

16-oz. pkg. reduced-fat ground pork sausage

1 c. onion, chopped

12-oz. can evaporated milk

1 c. skim or 2% milk

1 c. water

15-oz. can corn

14-3/4 oz. can creamed corn

1 russet potato, peeled and diced

salt and pepper to taste

CHICKEN & STARS SOUP

CLAUDIA KELLER
CARROLLTON, GA

This recipe is my secret weapon whenever one of the kids comes down with sniffles. Can't beat a big crock full of made-from-scratch chicken soup for chasing the chills!

4 to 6 chicken thighs
4 carrots, peeled and sliced
4 stalks celery, sliced
1 onion, peeled and halved
2 cloves garlic, minced
2 bay leaves
1 t. salt
1/4 t. pepper
6 c. water
2 cubes chicken bouillon
1/2 c. small star pasta, uncooked
Optional: 1/4 c. fresh parsley, chopped

Remove skins from chicken thighs, if desired. Arrange chicken in a 6-quart slow cooker. Add vegetables, garlic, bay leaves, salt and pepper. Add water and bouillon cubes; stir. Cover and cook on low setting for 7 to 8 hours, or on high setting for 4 to 5 hours, until chicken is cooked through. About 20 minutes before serving, transfer chicken to a bowl; discard onion and bay leaves. Turn slow cooker to low setting, if needed. Stir in pasta; cover and cook until tender, 15 to 18 minutes. Shred chicken; stir into soup along with parsley, if desired.

Makes 6 servings.

KITCHEN TIP

To keep a pot from boiling over, simply lay a wooden spoon across the top of the pot, like a bridge.

ALICE'S HAMBURGER STEW

JOALICE PATTERSON–WELTON
LAWRENCEVILLE, GA

*I got this recipe from my late Mom. It is a family favorite, especially
on cold winter or chilly fall evenings. An easy meal to prepare!
Serve with cornbread for a tasty meal.*

In a large skillet over medium heat, brown beef with
onion in oil. Drain well; set aside. Meanwhile, in a
Dutch oven over medium heat, combine carrots and
2 cups water. Bring to a boil; cook for 5 minutes. Add
potatoes and remaining water; cook until vegetables
are fork-tender. Add beef mixture, tomato paste and
seasonings. Simmer for 15 minutes.

Serves 12.

1 lb. ground beef chuck

1 c. onion, chopped

2 T. olive oil

4 c. carrots, peeled and
sliced 1-inch thick

4 c. water, divided

5 c. baking potatoes,
peeled and cut into
1-inch cubes

3 T. tomato paste

1 t. salt

1/2 t. pepper

MONK'S BEAN SOUP

STACI MEYERS
MONTEZUMA, GA

*My cousin Monk came to visit once and brought us a pot of this
yummy soup. I wouldn't let him leave until he shared the recipe!*

Combine ham hocks and water in a large soup pot.
Simmer over medium heat for 15 to 30 minutes. Melt
butter in a skillet; add onion and seasonings. Cook
for about 5 minutes, just until onion is tender. Place
beans in a slow cooker; add onion mixture, then pour
meat and broth over top. Cover and cook on high
setting for 4 to 6 hours, until beans are as tender as
desired. Shortly before serving time, dice meat from
ham hocks and stir back into slow cooker.

Makes 8 servings.

1 to 2 smoked ham hocks

6 to 8 c. water

2 T. butter

1 onion, chopped

3 to 5 T. dill weed

seasoned salt and
pepper to taste

16-oz. pkg. dried Great
Northern beans

FILÉ CHICKEN & SAUSAGE GUMBO

BETTY KOZLOWSKI
NEWNAN, GA

This is the meal we came home to from church every Sunday. Though there are many variations, my grandmother's and mom's gumbo was simple, yet unbelievably good.

1/4 c. oil
3 T. all-purpose flour
10 c. water
1-1/2 lbs. chicken pieces
1 lb. smoked pork sausage, sliced
1/4 c. onion, chopped
1/4 c. shallots, chopped
1/4 c. fresh parsley, chopped salt to taste
cooked rice

Combine oil and flour in a large soup pot over low heat. Cook over low heat, stirring constantly, until mixture is dark brown. Be careful not to allow it to burn. Slowly stir in water until mixture is smooth. Add remaining ingredients except rice. Bring to a boil over high heat; reduce heat to medium-low. Cover and simmer for one to 2 hours, stirring often. If desired, debone chicken and return meat to the pot. Serve over cooked rice.

Makes 6 servings.

BABA'S MILK SOUP

STACI PRICKETT
MONTEZUMA, GA

I have fond memories of this soup. When I was little, my Baba often made this Polish recipe for me for breakfast or as a snack. Baba always made it with noodles, but rice or oats are sometimes used.

4 c. milk
2 t. sugar
1 t. salt
2 to 3 c. kluski or medium egg noodles, uncooked
Garnish: 4 to 8 T. butter

In a large saucepan over medium heat, mix together milk, sugar and salt. Bring to a simmer but do not boil. Stir in noodles; simmer until tender. Ladle soup into bowls; top each bowl with one to 2 tablespoons butter.

Makes 4 servings.

Georgia

STUFFED BEER BRATS

STACI PRICKETT
MONTEZUMA, GA

I got this recipe from my dad. He didn't often cook for us, but when he did, dinner always seemed extra delicious.

Melt butter in a Dutch oven over medium heat. Add onion; cook for 3 minutes. Add brats and beer; bring to a boil. Reduce heat; simmer for 5 to 10 minutes. Remove brats to a plate, reserving beer mixture. Cut a V-shaped notch lengthwise in brats. Stuff with sauerkraut; wrap with bacon and fasten with a wooden toothpick. Grill over medium heat until golden and bacon is crisp. Return brats to beer mixture until served. Serve on buns, garnished as desired.

Serves 6.

1/4 c. butter, sliced
1 onion, sliced
6 bratwurst sausages
12-oz. can regular or non-alcoholic beer
15-oz. can sauerkraut, drained
6 slices bacon
6 hot dog buns, split
Garnish: Swiss cheese slices, horseradish mustard

TADPOLE HAM SOUP

SARA GOODROE
MOULTRIE, GA

A family recipe we've used for generations..The small onion pieces gave this wonderful southern dish its funny name.

Put ham cubes, pan drippings, onions and water into a soup pot. Bring to a slow boil over medium heat; simmer for 10 minutes. While soup is boiling, drop dumplings by tablespoonfuls into the pot. Slowly cook until dumplings are done, about 20 minutes. Add a little more water if soup seems too thick. Add pepper to taste.

Dumplings:
Combine egg and flour, working them together by hand until dough forms.

Serves 4.

2 c. cooked ham, cubed
1 c. pan drippings from a baked ham
4 to 5 green onions, cut into one-inch pieces
4 c. water
pepper to taste

DUMPLINGS
1 egg, beaten
1 c. self-rising flour

SMOKED TURKEY-MUSHROOM PANINI

DENISE WEBB
SAVANNAH, GA

I really enjoy panini sandwiches, so after trying an especially good one in a cute little cafe, I came home and tried to duplicate it. I think mine is even better than the one I had at the cafe...oh yum!

2 slices Vienna, Italian or rye bread

mayonnaise or Dijon mustard to taste

2 slices deli smoked turkey

1 slice provolone cheese

1 to 2 T. sliced mushrooms

2 to 3 T. fresh baby spinach

2 t. butter, softened

Spread one side of each bread slice with a small amount of mayonnaise or mustard. On one bread slice, layer turkey, cheese, mushrooms and spinach; top with second bread slice. Spread outside of sandwich lightly with butter. Place sandwich on a grill pan over medium-high heat; set a heavy pan or small skillet on top to weigh down the sandwich. Cook until golden; turn sandwich and repeat on the other side.

Makes one serving.

GARLICKY CHICKEN-MUSHROOM STEW

AMY BUTCHER
COLUMBUS, GA

Serve with prepared rice and a crispy salad...a winning combination.

4 boneless, skinless chicken breasts, cubed

salt and pepper to taste

10-3/4 oz. can cream of mushroom & roasted garlic soup

3/4 c. water

8-oz. pkg. whole mushrooms

1 c. baby carrots

2 stalks celery, chopped

Arrange chicken in a slow cooker; add salt and pepper to taste. Mix together soup and water; pour over chicken. Add mushrooms, carrots and celery; stir gently. Cover and heat on low setting 6 to 8 hours, until chicken juices run clear when pierced.

Serves 4.

PULLED BBQ CHICKEN BUNS

MARIE BENFIELD
CLARKESVILLE, GA

This is a real go-to recipe...it's so easy. Everyone I have shared it with enjoys it as much as I do. Serve with coleslaw and chips.

In a slow cooker, combine all ingredients except barbecue sauce and buns. Cover and cook on low setting for 6 to 8 hours, until chicken is tender. Drain off liquid. Shred chicken using 2 forks. Add desired amount of sauce; cover and cook another 30 minutes. Serve chicken on buns.

Makes 6 servings.

4 to 6 boneless, skinless chicken breasts
1/2 c. water
3 T. white vinegar
3 T. Worcestershire sauce
1 t. ground cumin
favorite barbecue sauce to taste
6 sandwich buns, split

FAMILY & FRIENDS CHICKEN SOUP

KAYLA HERRING
HARTWELL, GA

My family & friends request this soup when they aren't feeling well. It's an easy soup to toss together on a cold winter night.

Combine all ingredients except rice or noodles. Simmer until heated through. Stir in desired amount of cooked rice or noodles and serve.

Serves 6 to 8.

2 10-3/4 oz. cans cream of chicken soup
2 32-oz. containers chicken broth
2 13-oz. cans chicken, flaked
salt and pepper to taste
8-oz. pkg. thin egg noodles, or 2 boil-in bags instant rice, cooked

Georgia

GREEK PATTY POCKETS

LOUISE GREER
CARTERSVILLE, GA

These are the tastiest hot pockets you will ever eat...all the flavors and juices cook right into the bread. My favorite will always be Greek, but Mexican is a close second. Make 'em by the dozens, as they will keep in the freezer for several months. I guarantee these will be a hit for just about any kind of fall activities you enjoy.

1 lb. ground beef, chicken or turkey

1/2 c. onion, finely chopped

1 T. salt

1/2 T. pepper

garlic powder and ground coriander to taste

6 pita rounds

Garnish: crumbled feta cheese, sliced black olives, cucumbers, lettuce and tomatoes, Greek salad dressing

Combine meat, onion and seasonings. Mix well and form into 6 patties. Slice open each pita round; place a patty inside and press closed. Wrap packets tightly in aluminum foil; freeze. To serve, place wrapped packets on a baking sheet. Bake at 350 degrees for about 25 minutes, until hot and meat is cooked through. Serve with desired toppings on the side.

Mexican Patty Pockets Option:
Prepare, wrap, freeze and bake as above, using ground cumin instead of coriander and folded 8-inch corn tortillas instead of pitas. Serve with shredded Cheddar cheese, sliced black olives, lettuce and tomatoes, sour cream and salsa.

Makes 6 servings.

TERIYAKI BURGERS

JOANN
GOOSEBERRY PATCH

So simple! For parties, I like to make 8 mini burgers and serve them on Hawaiian slider buns. Jut cut the pineapple slices into wedges.

Form beef into 4 patties, 1/2-inch thick; season with salt and pepper. On a grill over medium-high heat, grill to desired doneness, 4 to 5 minutes per side. Brush with teriyaki sauce during the last 2 minutes of cooking. Grill pineapple for one to 2 minutes per side, brushing with sauce. Serve burgers in buns, topped with pineapple slices.

Makes 4 servings.

1-1/2 lbs. ground beef
1/2 t. salt
1/2 t. pepper
1/2 c. teriyaki sauce
4 pineapple slices
4 hamburger buns, split

SALLY'S CHICKEN PACKETS

KATHY COURINGTON
CANTON, GA

My best friend Sally gave me this recipe years ago and the kids really loved it. Very kid-friendly! Always a favorite in our house. It's a great way to use leftover chicken or turkey.

In a bowl, mix together chicken, cream cheese, milk, chives and salt; set aside. Separate crescents into 8 squares, pressing dough along perforated lines to seal. Spoon 1/4 cup chicken mixture onto each square. Fold over to form rectangles; press closed with a fork. Dip packets into melted butter and then into crushed croutons. Arrange packets on an ungreased baking sheet. Bake at 350 degrees for 20 to 30 minutes, until golden. Serve warm. Chicken filling may be made ahead of time, wrapped and frozen. To prepare, thaw overnight in the refrigerator.

Makes 8 servings.

2 c. cooked chicken, chopped
3-oz. pkg. cream cheese, softened
2 T. milk
1 T. fresh chives, chopped
salt to taste
2 8-oz. tubes refrigerated crescent rolls
1/4 c. butter, melted
1/2 c. seasoned croutons, crushed

CHILI CHEESE DOGS

BOOTSIE DOMINICK
SANDY SPRINGS, GA

Who doesn't love a good chili cheese dog with chips?

1 lb. ground beef chuck
1 c. onion, chopped
1 t. garlic, minced
15-oz. can tomato sauce
1 c. water
2 T. chili powder, or to taste
1/4 t. salt
1/4 t. pepper
8 hot dogs, cooked
8 hot dog buns, split and toasted
Garnish: shredded Cheddar cheese

In a large skillet over medium heat, combine beef, onion and garlic. Cook until beef is browned; drain. Stir in tomato sauce, water and seasonings. Bring to a boil; reduce heat to medium-low. Cover and simmer for 25 minutes, stirring occasionally. To serve, spoon chili sauce over hot dogs in buns; top with cheese.

Makes 8 servings.

MEDITERRANEAN TURKEY PITAS

TINA WRIGHT
ATLANTA, GA

Try marinated olive salad instead of the veggies for a different taste.

2 T. mayonnaise
2 whole-wheat pita rounds, halved
1/4 c. smoked deli turkey, sliced
1 c. marinated vegetable salad, drained and chopped
1/2 c. crumbled feta cheese

Spread mayonnaise inside pitas. Fill with turkey, vegetables and cheese.

Serves 2.

BBQ OVEN HOT DOGS

KATHY COURINGTON
CANTON, GA

My hubby loves hot dogs fixed this way! Tasty with a side of coleslaw and some crispy French fries.

Pierce each hot dog several times with a fork; arrange in a greased 13"x9" baking pan. Combine remaining ingredients in a bowl; spoon over hot dogs. Cover and bake at 350 degrees for one hour. Serve hot dogs on toasted buns, or as is.

Makes 8 servings.

1 lb. hot dogs
1/2 c. catsup
1/4 c. onion, minced
2 t. white vinegar
2 t. water
1-1/2 t. Worcestershire sauce
1 t. all-purpose flour
1 t. brown sugar, packed
1 t. paprika
1 t. chili powder
2 t. salt
1/4 t. pepper
Optional: 8 hot dog buns, split and toasted

HOMEY CHICKEN-LENTIL SOUP

CHANDRA CARVER
DANIELSVILLE, GA

I created this recipe to use up some leftover rotisserie chicken and other odds & ends from the pantry. It's super-easy to modify it to fit your personal tastes!

1-1/2 c. dried lentils

14-1/2 oz. can fire-roasted **Tex-Mex** style diced tomatoes

14-1/2 oz. can sliced carrots

15-oz. can corn

2 cubes chicken bouillon

1 to 2 T. ground cumin

1 t. red pepper flakes

2 T. dried, minced onion

2 cloves garlic, finely minced

3 to 4-lb. deli roast chicken, boned and shredded

Add all ingredients to a slow cooker. Add water to slow cooker until ingredients are just covered. Cover and cook on low setting for 5 to 6 hours, until lentils are tender.

Serves 6.

KITCHEN TIP

Keep your plastic wrap in the refrigerator. This will make the wrap stretch evenly and properly without sticking to itself.

CROCKERY MINESTRONE

DENISE WEBB
SAVANNAH, GA

We love soup...and this one is so easy, so delicious and makes the house smell so good while it cooks. It's one of our favorites!

In a skillet over medium heat, brown sausage in oil. Add sausage to a slow cooker; add tomatoes with juice and remaining ingredients except pasta. Cover and cook on low setting for 7 to 8 hours. About 20 minutes before serving, cook pasta according to package directions; drain. Add pasta to slow cooker. Cover and cook for 20 to 30 minutes longer. Remove bay leaves before serving. Ladle soup into bowls; garnish with Parmesan cheese.

Serves 12 to 15.

1/2 lb. sweet Italian pork sausage links, sliced

1 t. olive oil

28-oz. can diced tomatoes

15-oz. can cannellini beans, drained and rinsed

15-oz. can kidney beans, drained and rinsed

6 carrots, peeled and chopped

4 stalks celery, chopped

1 onion, chopped

6 sprigs fresh thyme

1/2 t. dried sage

2 bay leaves

1/2 t. salt

1/2 t. pepper

8 c. chicken broth

2 c. ditalini pasta, uncooked

Garnish: grated Parmesan cheese

CHEESY CAULIFLOWER SOUP

CONSTANCE BOCKSTOCE
DALLAS, GA

This soup is a healthy and delicious way to eat more vegetables. Loved by adults and children alike...a real comfort food.

1 head cauliflower, cut into flowerets

4 carrots, peeled and cut into bite-size pieces

2 T. dried celery flakes

2 t. no-salt herb seasoning

3 c. chicken broth

2 T. cornstarch

2 c. milk

8-oz. pkg. pasteurized process cheese, cubed, or 1 c. shredded Cheddar cheese

In a large stockpot over medium heat, combine cauliflower, carrots, celery, herb seasoning and chicken broth. Cook for 20 minutes, or until tender, stirring occasionally. In a small bowl, mix cornstarch into milk. Pour into stockpot; cook and stir until thickened. Fold in cheese; stir until melted.

Makes 4 to 6 servings.

JUST FOR FUN

A number of Georgia natives have achieved international recognition in literature. Alice Walker, whose novel "The Color Purple" (1982) won a Pulitzer Prize and was made into award-winning cinema and stage versions, and Margaret Mitchell, whose popular American Civil War epic "Gone with the Wind" (1936) was adapted into one of the great classics of American cinema.

CREAMY CHICKEN & DUMPLING NOODLE SOUP

SHARON PIRKLE
DOUGLASVILLE, GA

Homestyle comfort in a soup pot!

Place chicken in a soup pot; cover with water. Simmer over medium heat until tender, about 30 minutes. Cool chicken and dice; reserve 2 to 3 cups chicken broth in pot. Meanwhile, cook noodles according to package directions; drain. Add noodles, chicken, evaporated milk and seasoned salt to reserved broth. Simmer over low heat, stirring occasionally, for about 30 minutes.

Serves 6 to 8.

4 boneless, skinless chicken breasts
12-oz. pkg. dumpling noodles, uncooked
2 12-oz. cans evaporated milk
seasoned salt to taste

MINTED SPRING PEA SOUP

TINA WRIGHT
ATLANTA, GA

I like to serve this delicate soup topped with a dollop of Greek yogurt and a sprig of fresh mint.

In a large saucepan over medium heat, sauté onion in butter. Add broth; bring to a boil. Add frozen peas; return to a boil. Add mint; stir until mint is wilted. With an immersion blender, purée soup to desired consistency; season with salt and pepper. Serve warm or chilled.

Makes 4 servings.

1 c. onion, chopped
2 T. butter
2 c. chicken broth
2 c. frozen baby peas
3/4 c. fresh mint, chopped
salt and pepper to taste

CHAPTER FOUR

GEORGIA-ON-MY-MIND
Mains

FILL THEM UP WITH A STICK-TO-

THE-RIBS MEAL THAT IS FULL

OF FLAVOR AND HEARTY

ENOUGH TO SATISFY EVEN THE

BIGGEST APPETITE.

CHICKEN & PEACHES

THERESA LONG
ARNOLDSVILLE, GA

My mom used to make this delicious dish. People were never sure about the combination until they tried it, and then they always loved it, especially the warm biscuits on the top.

1/4 c. oil
1 t. butter, melted
1 c. all-purpose flour
1/2 c. milk
2 eggs, beaten
8 bone-in chicken thighs
  or 6 chicken breasts
garlic salt, salt and
  pepper to taste
15-1/4 oz. can sliced
  peaches in heavy syrup
16.3-oz. tube
  refrigerated flaky
  biscuits

Spread oil and melted butter in the bottom of a 3-quart casserole dish; set aside. Add flour to a shallow bowl; whisk together milk and eggs in a separate bowl. Roll chicken pieces in flour, then in egg mixture, then in flour again. Arrange chicken in casserole dish; sprinkle with seasonings. Bake, uncovered, at 400 degrees for 30 minutes, or until chicken is turning golden. Spoon peaches and syrup over chicken. Arrange biscuits in dish, pushing them down into drippings. Bake for another 12 to 15 minutes, until biscuits are golden and chicken juices run clear.

Makes 4 to 6 servings.

PRESENTATION

A basket filled with different kinds of rolls and loaves of French bread is a simple and tasty centerpiece for a pasta dinner.

Maple Ham & Eggs Cups, p8

Whether you are looking for a quick breakfast to start the day off right, no-fuss party fare for those special guests, satisfying soups and sandwiches for the perfect lunch, main dishes to bring them to the table fast, or a sweet little something to savor at the end of the meal, you'll love these recipes from the amazing cooks in beautiful Georgia.

Cathy's Scotch Eggs, p19

Apple Breakfast Cobbler, p27

Maple-Pecan Brunch Ring, p13

Grab & Go Breakfast Cookies, p11

Garlicky Baked Shrimp, p98

A Little Different Macaroni Salad, p37

Provincial Chicken, p94

Red Beans & Rice, p100

Mile-High Buttermilk Biscuits, p9

Hamburger Noodle Casserole, p92

One-Dish Speedy Couscous, p96

Layered Caribbean Chicken Salad, p36

Easy Georgian Peach Pie, p131

Paprika Chicken, p97

Asian Lettuce Wraps, p101

Quick & Spicy Shrimp Linguine, p108

ggie's Kickin' King Ranch Chicken, p90

Salmon Party Log, p121

Easy Chili Rellenos, p95

Debby's Orange Sherbet Cake, p141

Slow Peach Cobbler, p138

Southern Chicken & Dumplings, p95

Veggie & Sprouts Bagel, p20

Spareribs with Smoky Tomato BBQ Sauce, p

HOT CHICKEN SALAD

JOALICE PATTERSON–WELTON
LAWRENCEVILLE, GA

This has been a favorite family hand-me-down recipe for many years. I got it from my late mom, who was a fabulous Southern cook. I never met a dish of Mom's that I didn't like!

In a bowl, mix together all ingredients except potato chips, adding salt and pepper to taste. Spread in a greased 13"x9" baking pan; top with crushed chips. Bake, uncovered, at 375 degrees for 15 to 20 minutes. until hot and bubbly.

Serves 6 to 8.

5 boneless, skinless chicken breasts, cooked and diced

2 10-3/4 oz. cans cream of chicken soup

10-3/4 oz. can cream of celery soup

1-1/2 c. mayonnaise

1-1/2 c. celery, chopped

1-1/2 c. onion, chopped

2-1/4 oz. pkg. slivered almonds

5 T. lemon juice

1-1/2 c. sharp Cheddar cheese salt and pepper to taste

3 c. potato chips, crushed

SOUTHWEST TURKEY CASSEROLE

BETTY KOZLOWSKI
NEWNAN, GA

A great way to enjoy leftover turkey, and it can either be baked or cooked in a slow cooker! Your family will love it.

In a large saucepan, combine all ingredients except cheese. Cook over medium heat, stirring occasionally, until heated through. Spread half of mixture in a greased 1-1/2 quart casserole dish; top with half of cheese. Repeat layers. Bake, uncovered, at 350 degrees for 20 to 25 minutes, until hot and bubbly. For a slow cooker, omit stovetop step; layer as above in a 4-quart slow cooker. Cover and cook on high setting for one to 2 hours.

Makes 4 servings.

1 c. cooked turkey, cubed

6 corn tortillas, cut into 1-inch pieces

10-3/4 oz. can cream of chicken soup

4-oz. can chopped green chiles

1/2 c. sour cream or plain yogurt

1 c. corn

1/2 c. onion, chopped

1/2 c. shredded Cheddar cheese, divided

JUST FOR FUN

The Varsity in downtown Atlanta is the world's largest drive-in restaurant. It covers two city blocks, with space for 800 diners inside and 600 cars in the lot. Open since 1928, the restaurant serves around 15,000 people a day and they start every guest's dining experience with the famous greeting, "What'll ya have...what'll ya have?!"

MAGGIE'S KICKIN' KING RANCH CHICKEN

MAGGIE JO TUCKER
HARTSFIELD, GA

I got this recipe from my dear friend Aunt B, but I have adapted it to fit our tastes!

5 to 6 boneless, skinless chicken breasts, cooked and cubed

2 10-3/4 oz. cans cream of chicken soup

2 10-3/4 oz. cans cream of mushroom soup

2 10-oz. cans diced tomatoes with green chiles

1 T. chili powder

2 t. garlic salt

1-1/3 c. water

salt and pepper to taste

2 18-oz. pkgs. restaurant-style tortilla chips, divided

2 12-oz. pkgs. shredded Cheddar cheese

In a large bowl, combine chicken and remaining ingredients except chips and cheese; mix well. Place chips in a single layer in the bottom and up the sides of an ungreased 15"x10" baking pan; reserve any remaining chips. Spoon chicken mixture over chips. Cover with cheese. Bake, uncovered, at 350 degrees for 30 minutes, or until bubbly. Serve with remaining chips.

Serves 8 to 10.

KITCHEN TIP

Place a damp paper towel or two under your cutting board to keep it from moving around while you slice and dice.

EASY CHEESY RATATOUILLE

AMY BUTCHER
COLUMBUS, GA

When I first had this at a church potluck, I made sure to go back for seconds and to ask for the recipe!

Sauté vegetables with vinaigrette in a large oven-safe skillet over medium heat. Add tomatoes with juice; cook for 15 minutes. Sprinkle with cheeses. Bake, uncovered, at 350 degrees for 15 minutes, or until vegetables are tender.

Serves 6 to 8.

1 eggplant, peeled and cut into 1-inch cubes

1 onion, diced

1 red pepper, diced

1 zucchini, cut into 1-inch cubes

1/4 c. sun-dried tomato vinaigrette

14-1/2 oz. can diced tomatoes

1/4 c. grated Parmesan cheese

1 c. shredded mozzarella cheese

MEXICAN LASAGNA

AMANDA MELANCON
HAHIRA, GA

My daughter and I love this...plus we always have all the ingredients on hand!

1 lb. ground beef
1-1/4 oz. pkg. taco seasoning mix
8-oz. pkg. 10-inch flour tortillas
8-oz. pkg. cream cheese, softened and divided
1 c. shredded Cheddar cheese, divided
8-oz. can tomato sauce, divided

Brown beef in a skillet over medium heat; drain. Add taco seasoning and cook according to package directions. Spread 2 tortillas with 1/4 of the cream cheese and place cheese-side 27 up in an ungreased 13"x9" baking pan; spoon 1/4 of the beef mixture over tortillas. Top with 1/4 the shredded cheese and 1/4 the tomato sauce. Repeat layers 3 more times, ending with cheese. Bake, uncovered, at 350 degrees for about 25 minutes, or until heated through and cheese is melted.

Serves 4 to 6.

HAMBURGER NOODLE CASSEROLE

GLORIA KIRKLAND
PEARSON, GA

This is a quick & easy recipe that uses basic ingredients, comes together in a snap and tastes so good.

16-oz. pkg. wide egg noodles, uncooked
1-3/4 lbs. lean ground beef
1 onion, chopped
1 green pepper, chopped
1 t. salt
1 t. pepper
26-oz. can cream of mushroom soup
12-oz. pkg. shredded Cheddar cheese

Cook noodles according to package directions. Drain; set aside. Meanwhile, in a skillet over medium heat, brown beef with onion, green pepper, salt and pepper; drain. Combine beef mixture, noodles and soup. Pour into a greased 13"x9" baking pan; top with cheese. Bake, uncovered, at 325 degrees for 10 to 15 minutes, until cheese is melted and bubbly.

Serves 6 to 8.

BAKED CHICKEN JAMBALAYA

VICKI HOLLAND
HAMPTON, GA

I came up with this dish on short notice to feed a bunch of hungry teenagers with what I had on hand. I was surprised at the great blend of flavors.

In a skillet over medium-high heat, sauté sausage in butter until browned. Add chicken to skillet with sausage. Transfer sausage mixture into a 13"x9" baking pan; add mixed vegetables, onion, celery and green pepper. Top with cheese and cover with aluminum foil. Bake at 350 degrees for about 30 minutes, or until veggies are crisp-tender and cheese is melted. Serve over pasta.

Serves 8.

1 lb. pkg. smoked beef sausage, sliced

1/4 c. butter

4 c. cooked chicken, cubed

16-oz. pkg. frozen mixed vegetables, thawed

1 onion, sliced

4 stalks celery, sliced

1 green pepper, thinly sliced

2 c. shredded mozzarella or Cheddar cheese

16-oz. pkg. bowtie pasta, cooked

PROVINCIAL CHICKEN

SHARI UPCHURCH
DEARING, GA

I've tweaked this recipe over the years...now it's just the way my family likes it!

4 boneless, skinless
  chicken breasts
2 15-oz. cans diced
  tomatoes
2 zucchinis, diced
10-3/4 oz. can cream of
  chicken soup
2 T. balsamic vinegar
1 T. dried, minced onion
2 T. dried parsley
1 t. dried basil
1 c. shredded Cheddar
  cheese
1/2 c. sour cream
cooked bowtie pasta

In a slow cooker, combine chicken, tomatoes with juice, zucchinis, soup, vinegar, onion and herbs. Cover and cook on low setting for 6 to 8 hours. Remove chicken, cut into bite-size pieces and return to slow cooker. Stir in cheese and sour cream; cover and cook for an additional 15 minutes. To serve, spoon over cooked pasta.

Serves 6.

SOUTHERN CHICKEN & DUMPLINGS

STEPHANIE LUCIUS
POWDER SPRINGS, GA

A scrumptious-tasting homemade dish...with almost no effort!

Pour soup into a slow cooker; add onion and chicken. Pour in enough water to cover chicken. Cover and cook on low setting for 6 to 8 hours, or on high setting for 4 to 6 hours. About 45 minutes before serving, turn slow cooker to high setting. Remove chicken with a slotted spoon; shred into bite-size pieces and return to slow cooker. Drop biscuit quarters into slow cooker; stir well. Replace lid and cook for 35 minutes more, or until dumplings are done. Stir and serve.

Serves 6 to 8.

- 3 10-3/4 oz. cans cream of chicken soup
- 1/4 c. onion, diced
- 6 boneless, skinless chicken breasts
- 3-3/4 c. water
- 3 12-oz. tubes refrigerated biscuits, quartered

EASY CHILI RELLENOS

BETTY KOZLOWSKI
NEWNAN, GA

My husband fell in love with this the first time he tasted it! It's a potluck pleaser too.

Spread butter in a slow cooker. Layer chiles and cheeses; add tomatoes with juice. Stir together eggs, flour and milk; pour into slow cooker. Cover and cook on high setting for 2 to 3 hours.

Serves 6.

- 2 t. butter
- 7-oz. can whole green chiles, drained and cut in strips
- 8-oz. pkg. shredded Cheddar cheese
- 8-oz. pkg. shredded Monterey Jack cheese
- 14-1/2 oz. can stewed tomatoes
- 4 eggs, beaten
- 2 T. all-purpose flour
- 3/4 c. evaporated milk

ONE–DISH SPEEDY COUSCOUS

LAUREL PERRY
LOGANVILLE, GA

This hearty and flavorful meal is ready in a flash! The orange juice adds a nice zing...plus it's a great way to use up leftover chicken.

- 12-oz. pkg. couscous, uncooked
- 2 c. cooked chicken, diced
- 1 zucchini, chopped
- 1 stalk celery, thinly sliced
- 1 carrot, peeled and grated
- 2 c. orange juice
- 1/4 c. fresh basil, chopped
- 2 green onions, finely chopped
- 1/2 t. salt
- 1/2 t. pepper

Combine couscous, chicken and vegetables in a large serving bowl; set aside. Bring orange juice to a boil in a saucepan over medium heat; stir into couscous mixture. Cover tightly with plastic wrap; let stand for 5 minutes. Sprinkle with remaining ingredients. Stir gently until evenly mixed.

Serves 4.

PRIMAVERA PASTA & VEGGIES

KATHY COURINGTON
CANTON, GA

I make this whenever we want to have a lighter, meatless supper. So quick & easy and yummy, good any time of year. It's a recipe you can change around and add what you like...sometimes I will add cooked chicken and mushrooms.

- 3 c. bowtie or rotini pasta, uncooked
- 2 c. broccoli and/or zucchini, chopped or sliced
- 1 to 2 carrots, peeled and cut into thin strips
- 10-3/4 oz can cream of mushroom or chicken soup
- 1/2 c. milk
- 1/4 c. grated Parmesan cheese
- 1 clove garlic, minced
- 1/8 t. pepper

Cook pasta according to package directions; drain. Meanwhile, in a large saucepan, combine remaining ingredients; mix well. Cook, uncovered, over medium heat until vegetables are tender, about 10 to 12 minutes. Stir in cooked pasta and heat through.

Makes 4 servings.

PAPRIKA CHICKEN

**STACI PRICKETT
MONTEZUMA, GA**

This is old Polish comfort food at its finest. One bite, and it'll warm you up from your head to your toes.

Heat oil in a large skillet over medium heat. Season chicken pieces with salt and pepper. Cook chicken in oil until golden, about 7 minutes per side. Remove chicken from pan; drain, reserving 1/4 of drippings in pan. Sauté onion and garlic in drippings until onion is translucent. Stir in tomato, green pepper, paprika and water. Return chicken to skillet; cover and simmer for 35 to 45 minutes. Remove chicken from skillet; set aside. Skim any excess fat from the top. Mix together sour cream and flour; stir into tomato mixture. Stirring constantly, bring mixture to a boil. To serve, top noodles with chicken and ladle sauce over top.

Serves 4 to 6.

2 T. oil
3 to 4 lbs. chicken
salt and pepper to taste
1 onion, chopped
1 clove garlic, minced
1 tomato, chopped
1 green pepper, chopped
1-1/2 T. paprika
1/2 c. water
1 c. sour cream
1 T. all-purpose flour
cooked wide egg
   noodles

GARLICKY BAKED SHRIMP

AMY BUTCHER
COLUMBUS, GA

Everyone loves shrimp and this recipe will become your favorite way to serve it!

2 lbs. uncooked large
  shrimp, rinsed and
  unpeeled
1/3 c. white wine
  vinegar
2 T. canola oil
1 T. green onion, minced
1-1/2 T. pepper
2 cloves garlic, pressed
2 lemons, halved
1/4 c. fresh parsley,
  chopped
1 T. butter

Place first 6 ingredients in a 13"x9" baking pan, tossing to coat. Squeeze juice from lemons over shrimp mixture and stir. Add lemon halves to pan. Sprinkle shrimp with parsley; dot with butter. Bake, uncovered, at 375 degrees for 25 minutes, stirring after 15 minutes. Serve warm.

Makes 6 servings.

SPARERIBS WITH SMOKY TOMATO BBQ SAUCE

JASON KELLER
CARROLLTON, GA

No need to precook the ribs in boiling water...your pressure cooker does the job for you! Just add coleslaw and a pot of baked beans for a fantastic picnic meal.

Combine all ingredients for Smoky Tomato BBQ Sauce ahead of time; whisk until smooth and chill. Season ribs with salt and pepper; set aside. Choose the Sauté setting on the electric pressure cooker and heat oil until very hot. Working in batches, add ribs in a single layer; cook until browned on both sides, 5 to 7 minutes per batch, adding oil as needed. Transfer browned ribs to a plate. Add onion to drippings in pot and cook until soft, about 3 minutes. Return ribs to pot; add any juices from plate. Add water and sauce; toss to coat ribs. Press Cancel to reset pot. Secure lid and set the pressure release to Sealing. Choose Manual/Pressure and cook for 25 minutes at high pressure. Once cooking time is done, use Natural Release method to release pressure. Carefully open pot. Let stand for 15 minutes. Ribs should be falling-apart tender. Transfer ribs to a serving platter; skim fat from sauce and spoon over ribs. Combine all ingredients in a small bowl; whisk until smooth. Cover and refrigerate. Heat oil in a large skillet; brown pork on both sides. Add onion, peppers and garlic; cook and stir 5 minutes. Drain; add remaining ingredients. Cover and simmer 10 minutes, or until pork is tender.

Serves 6 to 8.

3-lb. rack pork spareribs, skin removed, cut into 2-rib serving-size portions
salt and pepper to taste
1 to 2 T. olive oil
1 onion, thickly sliced
1 c. water

SMOKY TOMATO BBQ SAUCE:
1 c. catsup
1/4 c. apricot preserves
1/4 c. cider vinegar
3 T. tomato paste
2 T. red wine or water
2 T. olive oil
2 T. soy sauce
1 T. dry mustard
1 T. onion powder
2 t. smoked paprika
1 clove garlic, pressed

RED BEANS & RICE

LAUREL PERRY
LOGANVILLE, GA

In this pressure-cooker recipe, you can switch up this recipe and use different kinds of beans such as black beans or navy beans with the rice for a different look and flavor. You can use brown rice as well.

4 slices bacon, cut into
    3/4-inch pieces
1/2 c. onion, chopped
1 stalk celery, chopped
1 green pepper, chopped
1 clove garlic, minced
1/2 t. cayenne pepper
1 c. long-grain rice,
    uncooked
2 15-oz. cans red kidney
    beans, drained
2 c. chicken broth
salt and pepper to taste

Select the Sauté function on the electric pressure cooker. When hot, cook the bacon until crisp. Remove bacon, reserving drippings in pot; set bacon aside. Add the onion, celery, pepper and garlic to the pot: sauté for 4 minutes. Stir in the cayenne and reserved bacon. Add the rice, beans and broth. Season with salt and pepper. Select Cancel to reset the pot. Close and lock the lid and set the pressure release to Sealing. Select Manual/Pressure and cook on high pressure for 5 minutes. Once the cooking is complete, use the Natural Release method for 10 minutes, then carefully release any remaining pressure manually using the Venting/Quick Release method. Open pot carefully. Serve immediately.

Serves 4.

JUST FOR FUN

At the top of Lookout Moutain, Georgia, from Lovers Leap, you can see seven different states.

ASIAN LETTUCE WRAPS

AMY BUTCHER
COLUMBUS, GA

Cooking pork in your electric pressure cooker is so easy and it shreds nicely for wraps or sandwiches of any kind. You can vary the spices you use to fit your liking.

Choose the Sauté function on electric pressure cooker and add oil, onion, garlic, ginger and mushrooms. Sauté about 2 minutes until mushrooms start to brown. Add the pork, broth, soy sauce, vinegar, pepper flakes and honey to the pot. Stir gently to mix; cook until browned, about 2 minutes. Press Cancel to reset pot. Set the pressure release to Sealing. Select Manual/ Pressure and cook for 35 minutes on high pressure. Once the timer is up, let the pot naturally release pressure for 10 minutes, then use Venting/Quick Release to release any remaining pressure. Remove pork and shred it; set aside. In a small bowl mix water and cornstarch. Choose the Sauté function and once the liquid in the pot is boiling, add the cornstarch mixture. Boil for one to 2 minutes, until the sauce has thickened. Add the pork back to the pot and stir well to coat. Press Cancel to reset pot. Serve pork on lettuce leaves. Garnish with green onion, sesame seeds and carrots.

Serves 8.

2 t. sesame oil

2 green onions, chopped

1 clove garlic, minced

1 T. fresh ginger, peeled and minced

8 oz. pkg. mushrooms, chopped

2 lbs. pork loin, cut into 2-inch chunks

1 c. chicken broth

1/3 c. soy sauce

1/3 c. balsamic vinegar

1/2 t. red pepper flakes

1 T. honey

2 T. cornstarch

3 T. water

large lettuce leaves such as bib or leaf lettuce

Garnish: green onions, sesame seeds, shredded carrot

BAKED CHICKEN & CHEESE PASTA

TINA WRIGHT
ATLANTA, GA

This was my Grandma Evelyn's tried & true potluck recipe for years! My family loves it too...it's a great way to enjoy that leftover turkey. Use elbow macaroni instead of ditalini, if you prefer.

3 c. ditalini pasta, uncooked
1/2 c. onion, chopped
1/2 c. celery, chopped
1/3 c. butter
1/3 c. all-purpose flour
2 T. chicken bouillon granules
4-1/2 c. whole milk
1-1/2 c. shredded sharp Cheddar cheese
3 c. cooked chicken, cubed
2-oz. jar diced pimentos, drained
2.8-oz. can French fried onions

Cook pasta according to package directions; drain. Meanwhile, in a large saucepan over medium heat, cook onion and celery in butter until tender. Stir in flour and bouillon; gradually stir in milk. Cook and stir until bubbly and thickened; remove from heat. Add cheese; stir until melted. Stir in cooked pasta, chicken and pimentos. Transfer to a greased 13"x9" baking pan. Cover and bake at 350 degrees for 30 minutes, or until hot and bubbly. Uncover and top with onions; bake another 5 minutes. Let stand 10 minutes before serving.

Serves 6 to 8.

CRANBERRY CHICKEN

BOOTSIE DOMINICK
SANDY SPRINGS, GA

This is an easy and delicious dish. I love to make it for my family and company at Christmastime. The ruby-red color looks so pretty on holiday china.

Arrange chicken breasts in a greased 13"x9" baking pan; set aside. Combine remaining ingredients except rice in a bowl; mix well and spoon over chicken. Cover with aluminum foil. Bake at 350 degrees for 30 minutes. Uncover and bake another 20 minutes, or until chicken juices run clear. Serve chicken and sauce over cooked rice.

Makes 4 to 6 servings.

4 to 6 boneless, skinless chicken breasts
15-oz. can whole-berry cranberry sauce
8-oz. bottle red Russian salad dressing
1-oz. pkg. onion soup mix
cooked rice

BASIL–MUSHROOM PIZZA

LAUREL PERRY
LOGANVILLE, GA

You may just have to make more than one...they're that good!

Melt butter in a large skillet over medium heat. Add mushrooms and garlic; sauté just until tender, about 5 minutes. Place crust on an ungreased baking sheet; brush with oil. Sprinkle spinach evenly over crust, followed by basil, cheese and mushroom mixture. Bake at 350 degrees for 8 to 10 minutes, or until cheese is melted and edges of crust are crisp.

Makes 4 servings.

2 T. butter
1 c. portabella mushrooms, sliced
2 cloves garlic, minced
12-inch Italian pizza crust
1 to 2 T. olive oil
1 c. spinach, sliced into 1/2-inch strips
1/2 c. fresh basil, chopped
8-oz. pkg. shredded mozzarella cheese

EASY-PEASY FANCY ZITI

**KELLY CRAVEN
SUGAR HILL, GA**

*Any time we have guests over for dinner, or if there is a family from
church in need of a meal, I toss this together. It's a meal that everyone
will eat, even the pickiest of eaters. Add a loaf of garlic bread and a
salad tossed with Italian dressing...you will feel like you are at a fancy
Italian restaurant! The best part is, you can make it your own with
ingredients that are your favorites.*

16-oz. pkg. ziti, rotini or
penne pasta, uncooked

14-oz. pkg. frozen mini
meatballs

2 24-oz. jars marinara
sauce, divided

16-oz. container ricotta
cheese

Optional: garlic salt to
taste

8-oz. pkg. shredded
mozzarella cheese

Cook pasta according to package directions; drain.
Meanwhile, add meatballs to a microwave-safe
bowl; microwave on high for 3 minutes. Remove
from microwave; cut meatballs into halves or thirds.
Spread some of the sauce over the bottom of a
lightly greased 13"x9" glass baking pan. Add cooked
pasta and meatballs to pan. Add ricotta cheese
by spoonfuls over pasta and meatballs. If needed,
smooth out the cheese over the dish. Sprinkle with
garlic salt, if desired. Spoon remaining sauce over
top; top with mozzarella cheese. Bake, uncovered,
at 350 degrees for 25 to 30 minutes, until bubbly and
cheese is golden.

Serves 6 to 8.

MOM'S BEEF STROGANOFF

DENISE WEBB
NEWINGTON, GA

I used to love walking into the house after school on a cold winter's day and smell this stroganoff cooking on the stove. And 50 years later, it's still one of my favorites...it is so comforting and delicious!

Brown beef in a large skillet over medium heat; drain. Blend in soup mix, flour, tomato paste and mushrooms. Stir in water; cover and simmer for 10 minutes. Stir in sour cream just before serving; Serve over cooked noodles.

Makes 4 to 6 servings.

- 1-1/2 lb. ground beef
- 1.35-oz. pkg. onion soup mix
- 3 T. all-purpose flour
- 2 T. tomato paste
- 8-oz. pkg. sliced mushrooms
- 2-1/2 c. water
- 1/2 c. sour cream
- cooked egg noodles

CHEESY PENNE BAKE

DENISE WEBB
NEWINGTON, GA

My dear daughter-in-law made this for us when we visited. It was so good and comforting. If you love pasta, this is for you.

In a large bowl, combine cooked pasta, browned beef, soup, sauce, seasonings and 2 cups cheese. Transfer to a greased 13"x9" baking pan; top with remaining cheese. Bake, uncovered, at 400 degrees for 25 to 30 minutes, until bubbly and cheese is melted.

Serves 6 to 8.

- 16-oz. pkg. penne pasta, cooked
- 1-1/2 lbs. ground beef, browned and drained
- 10-3/4 oz. can Cheddar cheese soup
- 30-oz. jar spaghetti sauce
- 1 t. Italian seasoning
- 1 t. pepper
- 3 c. shredded mozzarella cheese, divided

HERBED TURKEY BREAST

AMY BUTCHER
COLUMBUS, GA

*Brining is the secret trick that makes this turkey juicy and delicious!
It isn't hard at all, just a bit of prep ahead of time. Everyone at the
Thanksgiving dinner table will love it.*

9 c. water

3/4 c. salt

1/2 c. sugar

4 to 6-lb. bone-in whole
turkey breast, thawed
if frozen

1 onion, cut into 8
wedges

2 fresh rosemary sprigs

4 fresh thyme sprigs

3 bay leaves

6 T. butter, melted

1/4 c. chicken broth

In a 6-quart stockpot, combine water, salt and sugar; stir until salt and sugar are dissolved. Add turkey breast. Cover and refrigerate for 12 to 24 hours. Remove turkey, discarding brine; rinse thoroughly under cool running water and pat dry. Arrange onion and herbs on a rack in a large roasting pan. Place turkey on rack, skin-side up. In a bowl, combine butter and broth. Bake, uncovered, at 325 degrees for 1-1/2 hours; baste with butter mixture after one hour, and again after 30 minutes. Turn turkey skin-side down in pan. Bake another 30 to 60 minutes, continuing to baste, until a meat thermometer inserted in thickest part reads 165 degrees. Remove to a platter; let stand 15 minutes before carving.

Serves 8.

UPSIDE-DOWN PIZZA

KATHY COURINGTON
CANTON, GA

Years ago, a friend served this when we visited her. I loved it so much, she told me the recipe and we have enjoyed it as a family ever since. Easy and so good for entertaining or a potluck.

In a skillet over medium heat, brown sausage with onion; drain. Add pizza sauce, olives and mushrooms; cook until bubbly and spoon into a greased 13"x9" baking pan. Spread mozzarella cheese evenly over top. Combine eggs, milk, oil, flour and salt in a blender; process until smooth (or stir together in a bowl). Pour batter over mozzarella cheese; sprinkle with Parmesan cheese. Bake, uncovered, at 400 degrees for about 30 minutes, until puffed and golden. Cut and serve immediately.

Serves 6 to 8.

1 lb. mild Italian ground pork sausage

3/4 c. onion, chopped

15-1/2 oz. jar pizza sauce

4-oz. sliced black olives, drained

4-oz. can sliced mushrooms, drained

2 to 3 c. shredded mozzarella cheese

2 eggs, beaten

1 c. milk

1 T. oil

1 c. all-purpose flour

1/4 t. salt

1/4 c. grated Parmesan cheese

ZUCCHINI SPAGHETTI

KATHY COURINGTON
CANTON, GA

A different way to use your summer zucchini! It's easy to whip up on a busy night, and very good.

2 c. zucchini, diced
1/2 c. onion, diced
1/4 t. garlic, minced
1 T. olive oil
15-oz. can tomato sauce
1/4 c. water
1/4 c. grated Parmesan
  cheese
1 t. Italian seasoning
1 t. sugar
2 c. hot cooked spaghetti

In a skillet over medium heat, sauté zucchini, onion and garlic in olive oil for 5 minutes. Add remaining ingredients except spaghetti; mix well to combine. Stir in cooked spaghetti and simmer for 10 minutes, stirring occasionally.

Makes 4 to 6 servings.

QUICK & SPICY SHRIMP LINGUINE

LAUREL PERRY
LOGANVILLE, GA

Impress your family & friends with this easy-to-sauté classic recipe.

2 T. butter
2 cloves garlic, minced
14-1/2 oz. can spicy
  stewed tomatoes
1 lb. cooked, peeled large
  shrimp
1 red pepper, diced
2 green onions, chopped
8-oz. pkg. linguine
  pasta, cooked
Garnish: grated
  Parmesan cheese

Melt butter over medium heat in a large skillet. Add garlic; cook until golden, about one minute. Add tomatoes with juice; bring to a boil. Simmer uncovered, stirring occasionally, for 10 minutes, or until slightly thickened. Add shrimp, red pepper and green onions; cook for 5 minutes, until shrimp is heated through. Stir in hot pasta; toss until well coated. Garnish with Parmesan cheese.

Serves 4.

COMPANY CHICKEN & WILD RICE

DENISE WEBB
NEWINGTON, GA

You've got to try this! This dish is incredibly delicious and your guests will practically be licking their plates. I learned this simple recipe while my husband was in seminary, many years ago. It is still my favorite company dish!

In a large skillet over medium heat, brown chicken breasts on both sides in oil. Meanwhile, cook rice according to package directions. Add beans to cooked rice; transfer to a greased 13"x9" baking pan. Arrange chicken on top of rice mixture. Cover all with cheese and cream; cover tightly with aluminum foil. Bake at 350 degrees for one hour, or until chicken juices run clear.

Makes 4 servings.

4 boneless, skinless chicken breasts

1 to 2 T. oil

6-oz. pkg. long-grain and wild rice mix, uncooked

14-1/2 oz. can French-cut green beans, drained

1 c. shredded mozzarella cheese

1 c. whipping cream

GEORGIA PEACH SMOKED CHOPS

STACI PRICKETT
MONTEZUMA, GA

This recipe only has two ingredients, but it's a real tummy-pleaser! A great recipe for that next camping trip.

Grill pork chops over medium-high heat for 4 to 5 minutes on each side, just until browned. Place chops on a 24-inch length of heavy-duty aluminum foil. Spoon preserves over chops. Wrap in foil, forming a packet. Grill for another 10 to 15 minutes, until chops are heated through and glazed.

Makes 6 to 8 servings.

6 to 8 smoked pork chops

16-oz. jar peach preserves

SHRIMP & CONFETTI RICE

TINA WRIGHT
ATLANTA, GA

My older kids love to help put together these festive foil packets for dinner. Pop them in the oven and before you know it, it's time for dinner! In the summertime, these can be grilled on a covered grill for about 6 to 8 minutes.

1 lb. uncooked medium shrimp, peeled and cleaned
1-1/2 c. instant rice, uncooked
1/2 c. carrot, peeled and shredded
1/4 c. green onions, sliced
3/4 c. hot water
1/3 c. teriyaki marinade
2 t. sesame oil
1/2 t. garlic powder
Optional: 2 T. sliced almonds

In a large bowl, combine all ingredients except almonds; toss to mix well. Spoon 1/4 of shrimp mixture into the center of an 18-inch length of non-stick aluminum foil. Bring up sides of foil. Double-fold the top and ends to seal packet, leaving room for heat circulation inside. Repeat to make 3 more packets. Place packets on a large baking sheet; bake at 450 degrees for 15 to 18 minutes. Open packets carefully; sprinkle with almonds, if desired.

Makes 4 servings.

KITCHEN TIP

To quickly soften butter, warm a glass of water in the microwave, discard the hot water and wipe out the glass with a dry towel. Then turn the glass over top of the butter on a plate. The butter will begin softening immediately.

CHEESY PIEROGIE BAKE

DEANNE CORONA
HAMPTON, GA

On cold days, this dish puts smiles on my roommates' faces. They're always asking me, "When are you going to cook the pierogie cheesy stuff?" It's also a hit at my church family's fall potluck, and as a side for Christmas dinner.

Cook pierogies according to package directions; drain. Meanwhile, brown sausage in a saucepan over medium heat; drain. In a bowl, combine remaining ingredients; whisk until smooth, about 4 to 6 minutes. Stir in pierogies and sausage; transfer to a lightly greased 13"x9" baking pan. Bake, uncovered, at 350 degrees for 25 minutes, or until hot and bubbly.

Makes 4 servings.

16-oz. pkg. frozen potato or onion pierogies, uncooked

8-oz. pkg. ground pork, chicken or turkey sausage

1/2 c. chicken broth

3-oz. pkg. cream cheese

1 c. shredded Cheddar cheese

1/2 t. pepper

HADDOCK & CREAMY DILL SAUCE

CLAUDIA KELLER
CARROLLTON, GA

We've been trying to eat more fish lately, so I was happy to find this recipe. It's perfect with tiny new potatoes and grilled asparagus.

Brush fish with oil; season with salt and pepper. Place on a lightly oiled grate over medium heat. Grill for about 4 minutes on each side, turning once, until fish flakes easily with a fork. Stir together remaining ingredients except garnish. Serve fillets topped with sauce; garnish as desired.

Serves 4.

1 lb. haddock fillets

1 T. olive oil

salt and pepper to taste

1/2 c. sour cream

1 T. fresh dill, chopped

1 t. lemon juice

Garnish: fresh dill sprigs, thinly sliced lemon

TURKEY MEATLOAF WITH CRANBERRY GLAZE

PENNY SHERMAN
CUMMING, GA

I like to change things up each year for Christmas dinner. I made this recipe last year and discovered it's such a yummy alternative to traditional holiday fare!

14-oz. can jellied cranberry sauce, divided
1/2 c. chili sauce or catsup
1-1/4 lbs. lean ground turkey
1/2 lb. ground pork
1 egg, beaten
1 c. soft bread crumbs
1 onion, finely chopped
3/4 t. poultry seasoning
1/2 t. salt
1/8 t. pepper

Mix together 1/3 cup cranberry sauce and chili sauce or catsup. In a bowl, combine turkey and remaining ingredients. Add 1/3 of cranberry sauce mixture. Mix until well blended. Spoon into an 8"x4" loaf pan that has been sprayed lightly with non-stick vegetable spray. Bake, uncovered, at 350 degrees for one hour. Top with remaining cranberry sauce mixture and bake an additional 10 minutes. Let stand for 10 minutes before slicing. Serve with remaining cranberry sauce.

Serves 6.

GARLIC CHICKEN ALFREDO

LAUREL PERRY
LOGANVILLE, GA

Even picky eaters will love this creamy dish. And you'll love how easy it is!

16-oz. jar garlic Alfredo sauce, divided
4 to 6 boneless, skinless chicken breasts
4-oz. can sliced mushrooms, drained
cooked spaghetti or fettuccine pasta
Garnish: grated Parmesan cheese

Pour half of sauce into a slow cooker. Place chicken on sauce; top with mushrooms and remaining sauce. Cover and cook on low setting for 6 to 8 hours. Serve over pasta; garnish with Parmesan cheese.

Serves 4 to 6.

GRAN JAN'S CHICKEN PIE

JAN MORTON
HAWKINSVILLE, GA

This is a special favorite of my boys. It's easy to make if you start with a rotisserie chicken from the deli. It's delicious just the way it is, but add a drained can of mixed vegetables if you wish. Serve with steamed broccoli in cheese sauce.

Place chicken in a 13"x9" baking pan coated with non-stick vegetable spray. Whisk together soup, broth and cornstarch; pour over chicken. Whisk together remaining ingredients; pour evenly over chicken mixture. Bake, uncovered, at 400 degrees for 40 minutes, or until golden.

Serves 8 to 10.

- 4 c. cooked chicken, chopped
- 10-3/4 oz. can cream of chicken soup
- 1-1/2 c. chicken broth
- 2 T. cornstarch
- 1-1/2 c. self-rising flour
- 1 c. buttermilk
- 1/2 c. butter, melted

CREAMED BEEF OVER BISCUITS

STACI MEYERS
MONTEZUMA, GA

I was raised on this delicious recipe. It cooks up quickly from just a few simple ingredients...try it!

Brown beef in a skillet; drain. Add butter and one cup milk to skillet. Simmer over medium heat until butter is melted. Combine remaining milk with flour. Mix well until smooth; pour over beef mixture in skillet. Add salt and pepper; stir well. Reduce heat to medium-low and simmer for 3 to 5 minutes, until thickened. Serve over split biscuits.

Serves 4.

- 1 lb. ground beef
- 1/4 c. butter
- 12-oz. can evaporated milk, divided
- 1 T. all-purpose flour
- salt and pepper to taste
- 10-oz. tube refrigerated biscuits, baked and split

SPICY CHICKEN TENDERS

DANIELLE FISH
ACWORTH, GA

One night I created this dish for my husband, Ryan, and he ate his dinner so fast, he was asking for seconds! I serve it with roasted broccoli and cauliflower for a complete meal.

3/4 lb. boneless chicken tenders
1 T. olive oil
3 T. reduced-sodium soy sauce
Optional: 1 c. sliced mushrooms
1 to 1-1/2 t. red pepper flakes
cooked rice

In a skillet over medium-high heat, cook chicken in oil until golden. Stir in remaining ingredients except rice, adding red pepper flakes to taste. Let simmer until chicken is cooked through. Serve over cooked rice.

Makes 2 to 3 servings.

DEBBY'S CHICKEN LASAGNA

DEBBY CONAWAY
ROME, GA

This delicious recipe takes just four hours...pretty fast for a slow-cooker recipe. It's great when the holidays are hectic and you are in a pinch for time. Feel free to double the recipe if your slow cooker is large enough.

3 boneless, skinless chicken breasts, cooked and shredded
26-oz. jar spaghetti sauce
9-oz. pkg. lasagna noodles, uncooked and divided
1 c. ricotta cheese, divided
1 c. shredded mozzarella cheese, divided
1 c. shredded Cheddar cheese

In a bowl, mix chicken with sauce. Layer in an oval slow cooker as follows: 1/3 of chicken mixture, 1/3 of uncooked noodles, 1/3 of ricotta cheese and 1/3 of mozzarella cheese. Break noodles to fit as they are added. Repeat layering twice; top with Cheddar cheese. Cover and cook on high setting for 3 hours. Turn setting to low; continue cooking for one hour, or until bubbly and noodles are tender.

Makes 8 servings.

CHICKEN–MUSHROOM HASH

PENNY SHERMAN
COLUMBUS, GA

If you like mushrooms, you'll love this made-from-scratch hash.

In a large skillet over medium heat, heat one tablespoon oil. Add onion, garlic and mushrooms. Cook, stirring occasionally, until mushrooms are golden, 5 to 7 minutes. Add chicken, thyme, 1/2 teaspoon salt and pepper to skillet. Cook, stirring frequently, until chicken is almost done, 3 to 4 minutes. Drain; transfer mixture to a bowl. Add remaining oil to skillet over medium-high heat. Add potatoes; cook without stirring for about 6 minutes. Sprinkle with remaining salt; stir potatoes and cook until crisp and dark golden, about 4 minutes. Stir in chicken mixture, cream and parsley; heat through.

Serves 4 to 6.

4 T. oil, divided
1 onion, chopped
2 cloves garlic, chopped
1/2 lb. mushrooms, chopped
1-1/4 lbs. boneless, skinless chicken breasts, cubed
1/2 t. dried thyme
1 t. salt, divided
1/4 t. pepper
2 lbs. potatoes, peeled, cubed and cooked
1/4 c. whipping cream
2 T. fresh parsley, chopped

CHAPTER FIVE

SCOUT'S HONOR

Appetizers & Snacks

WHETHER YOU ARE HAVING

COMPANY OR JUST NEED A

LITTLE SNACK TO HOLD YOU OVER

UNTIL THE NEXT MEAL, YOU'LL

FIND THESE RECIPES ARE GREAT

FOR TAKING ON-THE-GO OR AS A

FAVORITE APPETIZER.

CAJUN CRAB DIP

DENISE WEBB
GUYTON, GA

My hubby and I always loved treating ourselves to this dip from the deli. Now I can make it myself. And mine is better...shhhh! Serve with crisp baguette slices or tortilla chips.

8-oz. pkg. cream cheese, softened
1/3 c. sour cream
1 T. hot pepper sauce
1-1/2 t. Worcestershire sauce
1-1/2 t. Cajun seasoning
1/2 t. Italian seasoning
1/2 t. garlic powder
1/2 c. shredded Cheddar cheese
3 green onions, chopped
8-oz. pkg. imitation crabmeat, flaked

In a large bowl, combine all ingredients except Cheddar cheese, green onions and crabmeat. With an electric mixer on medium speed, beat ingredients together well. Gently fold in cheese, onions and crabmeat. Cover and refrigerate for at least 2 hours.

Makes about 2 cups.

DARWIN CUPS

DENISE WEBB
NEWINGTON, GA

These are my go-to favorite appetizers. Our friend Darwin liked them so much that we named them for him. The rest is history! I'm sure you will love them, too.

Cook bacon in a skillet over medium heat until crisp; drain well and chop coarsely. Meanwhile, separate each biscuit horizontally into 3 thinner biscuits. Press each biscuit piece into a mini muffin cup, using a mini tart shaper if desired; set aside. In a bowl, combine bacon and remaining ingredients. Mix well; spoon mixture into biscuit cups. Bake at 375 degrees for 10 to 12 minutes, until golden and cheese is melted.

Makes 2-1/2 dozen.

8 slices bacon

10-oz. tube refrigerated flaky biscuits

3/4 c. shredded Swiss cheese

1/2 c. mayonnaise

3/4 c. ripe tomato, coarsely chopped

1/4 c. onion, coarsely chopped

1 t. dried basil

JUST FOR FUN

Scouting in Georgia has a long history, from the 1910s to the present day. The state is home to many milestones for the Scouting movement, including The Girl Scouts of America which was initiated by Juliette (Daisy) Gordon Low in Savannah, and President Jimmy Carter, who served as a Scoutmaster in Plains, Georgia.

AUNT KATHIE'S AWESOME PINEAPPLE CHEESE BALL

JENNIFER DORWARD
JEFFERSON, GA

We first tried this cheese ball many, many moons ago at my Aunt Kathie's house. We don't live near her anymore, but whenever Mom makes it, we think fondly of my aunt and my cousins, and all the good times we've had together.

2 8-oz. pkgs. cream cheese, softened

8-1/2 oz. can crushed pineapple, drained

1/2 green pepper, finely diced

2 T. onion, finely diced

1/2 t. salt

2 c. chopped walnuts, divided

snack crackers, sliced trail bologna or beef stick

In a large bowl, stir cream cheese until smooth. Blend in pineapple, green pepper, onion, salt and one cup walnuts. Shape into a ball; roll ball in remaining walnuts. Cover with plastic wrap and refrigerate overnight. Serve with crackers and sliced trail bologna or beef stick.

Makes 12 servings.

PRESENTATION

For pretty appetizer picks, stick two stickers with monogram initials, back-to-back on the tips of your toothpicks.

Georgia

SALMON PARTY LOG

PAULA BRASWELL
MARIETTA, GA

*This recipe can be made a day in advance and tucked into the fridge...
so handy when you're planning a party!*

Place all ingredients except pecans, parsley and crackers in a medium bowl. Mix thoroughly; shape into a log. Place pecans and parsley on wax paper; roll log in mixture until coated. Cover and chill at least 2 hours. Serve with crackers.

Makes about 3 cups.

16-oz. can salmon, drained and flaked
8-oz. pkg. cream cheese, softened
1 T. lemon juice
1 t. prepared horseradish
2 t. onion, grated
1/4 t. salt
1/4 t. Worcestershire sauce
1/2 c. chopped pecans
3 T. fresh parsley, chopped
water crackers

PECAN CHICKEN SALAD SPREAD

AMY BUTCHER
COLUMBUS, GA

*We do love our pecans here in Georgia! This flavorful spread is perfect
for snacking or for making tea sandwiches.*

In a bowl, combine all ingredients except crackers; mix well. Cover and chill. Serve with crackers or bread slices.

Makes 2-1/2 cups.

1-3/4 c. cooked chicken breast, finely chopped
1 c. chopped pecans
2/3 c. mayonnaise
1 stalk celery, chopped
1/2 c. onion, minced
1 t. salt
1/2 t. garlic powder
assorted crackers, French bread slices

RASPBERRY BARBECUE WINGS

TINA WRIGHT
ATLANTA, GA

I was looking for something to do with chicken wings and found this recipe. It was a hit!

2/3 c. barbecue sauce
2/3 c. raspberry jam
3 T. onion, finely chopped
1 to 2 jalapeño peppers, seeded and minced
2 t. garlic, minced and divided
2 t. smoke-flavored cooking sauce, divided
1/4 t. salt
3 lbs. chicken wings, separated
1 onion, sliced
1 c. water

In a bowl, combine barbecue sauce, jam, chopped onion, jalapeños, one teaspoon garlic, one teaspoon smoke flavoring and salt; mix well. Cover and chill at least 2 hours. Arrange chicken wings on a greased 15"x10" jelly-roll pan; top with sliced onion and remaining garlic. Combine water and remaining smoke flavoring in a cup; spoon over wings. Bake at 350 degrees for 35 to 45 minutes, until juices run clear. Transfer wings to a greased broiler pan; brush with sauce. Broil 4 to 6 inches from heat for 20 to 25 minutes; turn and baste every 5 minutes with sauce mixture.

Makes about 2-1/2 dozen.

JUST FOR FUN

As one of the original Thirteen Colonies, Georgia's history dates back more than 300 years. Throughout history there have been spooky stories about hauntings and spirit sightings throughout the Peach State.

Georgia

FRESH PEACH SALSA

DENISE WEBB
NEWINGTON, GA

We love our peaches here in Georgia! This is such a refreshing, beautiful salsa and so very good. Serve with tortilla chips, or spoon over grilled chicken.

In a bowl, stir together all ingredients. Cover and chill for one to 2 hours before serving.

Makes 2 cups.

2 c. peaches, peeled, pitted and chopped

1/4 c. sweet onion, chopped

1 clove garlic, minced

3 T. lime juice

1 to 3 jalapeño peppers, finely chopped and seeded

1 T. fresh cilantro, snipped

1/2 t. sugar

CHICKEN RANCH DIP

TINA MATIE
ALMA, GA

This is a recipe that my family loves. We always make this for our Christmas get-together. It's really good with scoop-type tortilla chips, to scoop up every delicious bit!

In a large bowl, blend together cream cheese and salad dressing; set aside. Spread chicken in a lightly greased 13"x9" baking pan. Sprinkle chicken with hot sauce; spread cream cheese mixture over top. Sprinkle shredded cheeses on top. Bake, uncovered, at 350 degrees for 20 to 25 minutes, until bubbly.

Makes 10 to 12 servings.

8-oz. pkg. cream cheese, softened

24-oz. bottle ranch salad dressing

3 13-oz. cans chicken breast, drained and flaked

1/2 to 1 6-oz. bottle hot pepper sauce, to taste

8-oz. pkg. shredded Monterey Jack cheese

8-oz. pkg. shredded Pepper Jack cheese

GARDEN HUMMUS DIP

CONSTANCE BOCKSTOCE
DALLAS, GA

This is both kid and grown-up friendly! I wanted to make my own hummus that would be more nutritious and lighter than those on the market. I now double the recipe and eat it more often. Delicious on avocado toast too.

16-oz. can chickpeas, drained

2 carrots, peeled and cut into chunks

2 stalks celery with leaves, cut into chunks

2 T. olive oil

1 t. onion powder

1 t. garlic powder

pepper to taste

snack crackers, tortilla chips or sliced vegetables

In a food processor, combine chickpeas, carrots, celery, oil and seasonings. Process until smooth, about 5 minutes. Transfer to a bowl; cover and refrigerate up to 7 days or freeze. Serve with crackers, tortilla chips or vegetables.

Makes 4 servings.

TOMATO-BACON CUPS

MICAELA BRADY
CUMMING, GA

This recipe is a huge family favorite...they are gone the moment I put them out on the counter!

8 slices bacon

16-oz. tube refrigerated buttermilk biscuits

1 ripe tomato, diced

1/2 yellow onion, diced

3/4 c. shredded Swiss cheese

1/2 c. mayonnaise

In a skillet over medium heat, cook bacon until crisp; set aside on paper towels. Meanwhile, split each biscuit horizontally into halves; press each half into a lightly greased muffin cup and set aside. In a bowl, combine crumbled bacon and remaining ingredients; mix well. Fill each biscuit with about a teaspoonful of mixture. Bake at 375 degrees for 10 to 12 minutes, until golden and cheese is melted.

Makes 2 dozen.

YVONNE'S CHILI DIP

BETTY KOZLOWSKI
NEWNAN, GA

This disappears quickly...my whole family loves this dip! The first time I tried it at a church potluck, I knew I had to get the recipe from Yvonne. She raised four boys and was used to providing hearty meals for them. Serve with scoop-type tortilla chips or corn chips.

Spread softened cream cheese in the bottom of an ungreased 13"x9" baking pan; set aside. Mix chili and cooked turkey or beef; spread over cream cheese. Top with shredded cheese. Bake, uncovered, at 350 degrees for 15 minutes, or microwave for 5 minutes, until cheese melts. Serve hot.

Serves 12.

- 2 8-oz. pkgs. low-fat cream cheese, softened
- 20-oz. can chili, no beans
- 2 lbs. ground turkey or beef, browned and drained
- 3 c. shredded Cheddar cheese

GRANNY'S CHEESE STRAWS

KAYLA HERRING
HARTWELL, GA

My Grandmother Betty often catered weddings or other events. These cheese straws were sure to be on the menu!

In a large bowl, blend cheese and butter; set aside. Sift remaining ingredients into another bowl; add to cheese mixture and mix well. Knead dough until smooth. On a floured surface, roll out small portions of dough at a time, 1/2 inch thick. Cut into strips, 1/4 inch wide and one inch long. Dough may also be rolled into one-inch balls and flattened with a fork. Place on parchment paper-lined baking sheets. Bake at 350 degrees for 12 to 16 minutes, until lightly golden.

Makes about 3 dozen.

- 2 8-oz. pkgs. shredded sharp Cheddar cheese
- 1/2 c. butter
- 2 c. all-purpose flour
- 1 t. baking powder
- 1 t. salt
- 1 t. sugar

ALL-TIME-FAVORITE RECIPES FROM GEORGIA COOKS **125**

LAYERED SALSA DIP

JULIE WARREN
VALDOSTA, GA

My family has enjoyed this yummy dip for years. It's so quick & easy. It's very showy to take to an event too. Serve with your favorite crunchy corn chips.

8-oz. pkg. sour cream, softened
1 c. favorite mild, medium or hot salsa
1 c. shredded Cheddar or Cheddar Jack cheese
Optional: chopped green onions or fresh parsley

Spread sour cream in a square or rectangular serving dish; spread salsa over sour cream layer. Sprinkle shredded cheese evenly over salsa. Garnish with chopped green onions or parsley, if desired. Cover and chill until serving time.

Makes 6 to 8 servings.

FROSTED CHEESE SQUARES

WANDA WILSON
HAMILTON, GA

Handed down for a couple of generations, this scrumptious cheesy recipe has been loved by everyone! This may be baked ahead and frozen, which is handy for busy days.

1 loaf day-old or frozen sliced sandwich bread
2 5-oz. jars sharp pasteurized process cheese spread
8-oz. can grated Parmesan cheese
3/4 c. butter
1 egg, beaten
1 t. Worcestershire sauce
1 lb. bacon, crisply cooked and crumbled
Optional: thinly sliced green olives with pimentos

With a serrated bread knife, trim crusts from bread slices; set aside. In a large bowl, combine remaining ingredients except optional olives; blend well. Spread cheese mixture between pairs of bread slices, making sandwiches. Cut each sandwich into 4 squares. Spread remaining cheese mixture over the top and edges of each square. Arrange on an ungreased aluminum foil-covered baking sheet. Bake at 350 degrees for 15 minutes, or until toasted. When cool, garnish each with 3 olive slices, if desired.

Makes about 4 dozen.

CRISPY OVEN WINGS

JASON KELLER
CARROLLTON, GA

My family loves these juicy wings so much, sometimes we have them for dinner. Serve with your favorite dipping sauce.

Pat chicken wings dry with paper towels; set aside. In a plastic zipping bag, combine remaining ingredients except butter. Shake to mix; add wings to bag and shake until well coated. Spread melted butter on an aluminum foil-lined rimmed baking sheet. Arrange wings on pan; turn to coat. Bake at 425 degrees for 30 minutes. Turn wings over and bake for another 15 minutes, or until crisp, golden and juices run clear when pierced.

Makes 20 pieces.

> 10 chicken wings, separated
> 1/3 c. all-purpose flour
> 1 T. paprika
> 1 t. garlic salt
> 1 t. pepper
> 1/4 to 1/2 t. cayenne pepper
> 3 T. butter, melted

MEXICAN TORTILLA ROLL-UPS

PAULA SUMMEY
DALLAS, GA

My daughter's second-grade school teacher gave me this tasty recipe many years ago. I have taken it to many potlucks and parties.

In a large bowl, combine all ingredients except tortillas and salsa; stir until well mixed. Spread mixture lightly onto tortillas. Roll up and wrap tightly with plastic wrap. Refrigerate overnight. At serving time, unwrap roll-ups and slice. Serve with salsa.

Makes about 2 dozen.

> 2 8-oz. pkgs. cream cheese, softened
> 2 4-oz. cans chopped green chiles, drained
> 2 3.8-oz. cans chopped black olives, drained
> 1 T. garlic powder
> 1 T. ground cumin
> 1 to 2 dashes hot pepper sauce
> salt and pepper to taste
> 10 flour tortillas
> Garnish: favorite salsa

CHAPTER SIX

CHRISTMAS TOWN
Desserts

THERE IS ALWAYS ROOM FOR
DESSERT. SO WHEN YOUR SWEET
TOOTH IS CALLING, THESE SIMPLE
SWEETS ARE THE PERFECT WAY TO
END THE DAY.

MOWE'S POUND CAKE

**KAYLA HERRING
HARTWELL, GA**

My Grandmother Bertie made this recipe for every Thanksgiving, Christmas and Easter. It is my mom's favorite cake, and she chose it for her birthday every year. My grandmother is no longer here, but we cherish her recipe and think of her often whenever we have a pound cake. The name of the recipe is Mowe's Pound Cake, because that's what I called her as a child.

2 c. butter or shortening
2-2/3 c. sugar
8 eggs
3-1/2 c. all-purpose flour
1/2 c. whipping cream
1 t. vanilla extract
1/2 t. lemon extract
1/2 t. almond extract

In a large bowl, stir butter or shortening until softened. Stir in sugar, a little at a time. Add eggs, one at a time, mixing well after each. Add flour, cream and extracts; mix well. Pour batter into a tube pan greased with shortening. Bake at 350 degrees for one hour and 40 minutes. Cool; turn out of pan and slice to serve.

Makes 16 servings.

DINNERTIME CONVERSATION

Babyland General Hospital, located two hours northeast of Atlanta, is home of the famous Cabbage Patch Kids. At the hospital you'll see dolls popping out of a cabbage patch in the ground and a nursery full of crying baby Cabbage Patch Kids. The main attraction at Babyland General Hospital is a huge "Mother Cabbage" tree, where all the Cabbage Patch Kids come from.

Georgia

EASY GEORGIAN PEACH PIE

JOANN
GOOSEBERRY PATCH

I've been making this pie for years, but only when the peaches are in season. It tastes like Heaven!

Line pie plate with one pie crust. Combine peaches with flour, sugar, spice, salt and lemon juice; mix lightly. Fill pastry with peach mixture and dot with butter. Top pie with second pie crust, crimp the edges and cut 5 to 6 one-inch slits in the top of crust for venting. Whisk egg yolk with water to create egg wash. Brush crust with egg wash and sprinkle with sugar. Bake at 400 degrees for 45 to 50 minutes or until juices are bubbling and the crust is golden. Serve warm with whipped cream or ice cream.

Serves 6 to 8.

2 9 to 10-inch pie crusts

6 c. fresh peaches, peeled, pitted and sliced

1 c. sugar

4 T. flour

1/2 t. cinnamon or apple pie spice

1/2 t. salt

2 t. lemon juice

2 T. butter

1 egg yolk

2 T. water

additional sugar for dusting

Garnish: whipped cream or vanilla ice cream

TRACEY'S PEAR CAKE

TRACEY GASAWAY
TRION, GA

This is a yummy recipe I used when the two pear trees in our yard were producing more pears than I knew what to do with. This cake freezes really well.

1 c. sugar
1 c. brown sugar, packed
3 eggs, beaten
1 c. oil
2 t. vanilla extract
3 c. all-purpose flour
1 t. salt
1 t. baking soda
2 t. cinnamon
4 c. pears, peeled, cored and sliced

TOPPING
1/2 c. butter
1/4 c. milk
1/2 c. brown sugar, packed

In a large bowl, mix all ingredients by hand in order given. Pour batter into a greased 13"x9" baking pan. Bake at 350 degrees for 45 minutes. Pour Topping over cake; return to oven for 4 minutes. Cut into squares.

Topping:
Combine all ingredients in a saucepan. Bring to a low boil for 3 minutes, stirring until brown sugar dissolves.

Makes 15 servings.

REINDEER DROPPINGS

**LINDA ROPER
PINE MOUNTAIN, GA**

*My children, grandchildren and friends love this tasty treat! I make
it every Christmas for family & friends and pack in candy tins. I
am asked for this recipe all the time. So rich and delicious...it will
disappear quickly!*

In a greased 6-quart slow cooker, combine peanuts,
white and milk chocolate chips and baking chocolate.
Cover and cook on low setting for 2 hours, or
until chocolate is melted. Stir well. Add remaining
ingredients; mix well. Drop mixture by tablespoonfuls
onto parchment paper-lined baking sheets; allow to
set. Store in an airtight container.

Makes 6 to 7 dozen.

16-oz. jar honey-roasted
peanuts

2 16-oz. pkgs. white
chocolate chips

12-oz. pkg. milk
chocolate chips

4-oz. pkg. German
chocolate baking
chocolate, broken

12-oz. pkg. butterscotch
chips

2 12-oz. pkgs. candy-
coated chocolates

12-oz. pkg. brickle toffee
baking bits

JUST FOR FUN

Santa Claus, Georgia loves Christmas so
much that it's named after jolly ol' Saint
Nick himself. Even the streets are holiday-
themed. You'll find a Santa's mailbox
outside of the Santa Claus City Hall
(located at 25 December Drive) and letters
receive a special Santa Claus postmark.

STRAWBERRY LAYER CAKE

STEVEN WILSON
CHESTERFIELD, VA

When I was growing up spring meant strawberry time, when I'd go with Grandma to pick those luscious berries. She always baked this delicious cake for the Sunday night church social.

6-oz. pkg. strawberry gelatin mix
1/2 c. hot water
18-1/2 oz. pkg. white cake mix
2 T. all-purpose flour
1 c. strawberries, hulled and chopped
4 eggs

In a large bowl, dissolve dry gelatin mix in hot water; cool. Add dry cake mix, flour and strawberries; mix well. Add eggs, one at a time, beating slightly after each one. Pour batter into 3 greased 8" round cake pans. Bake at 350 degrees for 20 minutes, or until cake tests done with a toothpick. Cool; assemble layers with frosting.

Strawberry Frosting:
Blend butter and powdered sugar together, adding sugar to desired consistency. Add strawberries; blend thoroughly.

Serves 12.

STRAWBERRY FROSTING

1/4 c. butter, softened
3-3/4 to 5 c. powdered sugar
1/3 c. strawberries, hulled and finely chopped

PUMPKIN CRISP

BOOTSIE DOMINICK
SUCHES, GA

My husband loves this dessert. It's great to serve at Thanksgiving or anytime in the fall. Serve topped with cinnamon or vanilla ice cream... yum!

Reserve one cup dry cake mix for topping. In a large bowl, combine remaining cake mix, 1/2 cup melted butter and one beaten egg. Press batter into the bottom of a greased 13"x9" baking pan; set aside. In another bowl, whisk together pumpkin, remaining beaten eggs, brown sugar, evaporated milk and spice. Spoon over batter in pan. In another bowl, combine reserved cake mix, remaining melted butter, sugar and nuts; sprinkle over pumpkin layer in pan. Bake at 350 degrees for 50 minutes. Serve warm or chilled.

Makes 8 to 10 servings.

18-1/4 oz. pkg. yellow
  cake mix, divided
3/4 c. butter, melted
  and divided
4 eggs, divided
29-oz. can pumpkin
1/2 c. brown sugar,
  packed
2/3 c. evaporated milk
2 t. pumpkin pie spice
1/2 c. sugar
1/4 c. chopped nuts

CHRISTMAS PLUM CAKE

KATHY COURINGTON
CANTON, GA

When my mother first made this, I asked her what it was, it was so good and rich! Easy too. A family favorite, great for the holidays.

In a large bowl, beat together sugar, oil and eggs, beating after each egg; set aside. In another bowl, mix together flour, spices and nuts. Add flour mixture to sugar mixture; mix well and stir in baby food. Pour batter into a greased and floured Bundt® pan. Bake at 350 degrees for one hour, or until a toothpick inserted near the center tests clean. Cool cake in pan; turn out onto a plate. Sprinkle with powdered sugar.

Serves 8 to 12.

2 c. sugar
1 c. oil
3 eggs
2 c. self-rising flour
1 t. cinnamon
1 t. ground cloves
1 c. chopped nuts
2 4-oz. jars plum baby
  food
Garnish: powdered
  sugar

BEE HIVE DESSERT

KATHY COURINGTON
CANTON, GA

Every Christmas my sister and I would request this dessert. It was always a family favorite and so festive...nice and light too after a heavy holiday meal. I hope you enjoy it too!

3.4-oz. pkg. instant
lemon pudding mix

2 c. milk

2 angel food cakes,
sliced and divided

16-oz. container frozen
whipped topping,
thawed

16-oz. jar maraschino
cherries, well drained
and halved

In a large bowl, whisk dry pudding mix and milk for 2 minutes, until thickened. Set aside for 5 minutes. Meanwhile, line a deep bowl with wax paper all the way to top. Use 1/3 of cake slices to line bowl to top. Spoon in half of pudding; top with another 1/3 of cake slices. Repeat layers, ending with cake. Cover and refrigerate 8 hours to overnight. To serve, invert bowl onto a serving platter; peel off wax paper. Cover with whipped topping; decorate all over with cherries. Return to refrigerator if not serving immediately. May also be layered in a 13"x9" glass baking pan.

Serves 12.

MAPLE CREAM CANDY

TINA GOODPASTURE
MEADOWVIEW, VA

I love this candy. It's simple to make, but has a big, sweet taste! Nuts may be added while beating, if desired.

1 c. pure maple syrup

1/2 c. whipping cream

1 c. sugar

1 T. butter

Combine all ingredients in a heavy saucepan. Cook over medium-low heat until sugar dissolves, stirring occasionally. Cook to soft-ball stage, or 234 to 243 degrees on a candy thermometer. Remove from heat; beat until cool and creamy. Pour into a buttered 8"x8" baking pan. Cool until set; cut into squares.

Makes 2 dozen.

SOUTH GEORGIA PECAN PIE

WENDY QUATTLEBAUM
MCDONOUGH, GA

I came across this recipe while going through some of my mother-in-law's old mementos. The recipe was written on a very small index card. I can just picture some woman in my husband's family, handwriting the card for a church potluck or recipe exchange. It warms my heart just thinking about it! I'm honored to have found the recipe. It's an honor to cook like the women who have come and gone before us. Use dark corn syrup for a thicker, richer taste.

Arrange pie crust in a 9" pie plate; loosely cover with aluminum foil. Bake at 350 degrees for 10 minutes, or until lightly golden; cool. Cook butter, corn syrup and sugar in a saucepan over medium heat for about 5 minutes, stirring often, until butter is melted and sugar is dissolved. Remove from heat. In a bowl, stir together eggs, vanilla and pecans; combine with butter mixture and stir well. Pour mixture into baked crust; cover loosely with foil. Bake at 350 degrees for 20 minutes; uncover and bake for another 10 minutes. Cool at room temperature or in the refrigerator for several hours before serving. Serve slices garnished as desired.

9-inch pie crust, unbaked
1/2 c. butter
1/2 c. light corn syrup
1 c. sugar
3 eggs, beaten
1 T. vanilla extract
1 c. chopped pecans
Garnish: whipped topping or vanilla ice cream

Makes 8 servings.

EASY APPLE POPOVERS

DEBRA COOGLE
OGLETHORPE, GA

These fruity treats are delish! I made up this recipe when I needed a dessert to carry to the family of a friend who had just come home from the hospital.

10-oz. tube refrigerated flaky biscuits
2 c. sweetened applesauce
1 c. powdered sugar
3 to 4 T. milk

Spray a muffin tin with non-stick vegetable spray. Separate biscuits. Press a biscuit into the bottom and partway up the sides of each muffin cup. Spoon applesauce into biscuits. Bake at 300 degrees for about 10 to 15 minutes, until biscuits are done. Remove popovers from muffin tin; let cool. Mix powdered sugar and milk to a drizzling consistency; drizzle over popovers.

Makes 10 servings.

SLOW PEACH COBBLER

LAUREL PERRY
LOGANVILLE, GA

This is a great dessert to share at potlucks! People won't believe that it was made in a slow cooker.

1/3 c. sugar
1/2 c. brown sugar, packed
3/4 c. biscuit baking mix
2 eggs, beaten
2 t. vanilla extract
2 t. butter, melted
3/4 c. evaporated milk
3 to 4 peaches, peeled, chopped and lightly mashed
3/4 t. cinnamon

Spray a slow cooker with non-stick vegetable spray. In a large bowl, combine sugars and baking mix. Add eggs, vanilla, butter and milk; stir well. Fold in peaches and cinnamon. Pour into slow cooker. Cover and cook on low setting for 6 to 8 hours, or on high setting for 3 to 4 hours. Serve warm.

Serves 6 to 8.

DOUBLE CRUNCH BARS

JAN STAFFORD
CHICKAMAUGA, GA

My friend, Debby, shared this recipe with me. Her 6 children and my 5 children all love these scrumptious bars!

Mix all ingredients together; press into a greased 15"x10" jelly-roll pan. Bake at 450 degrees for 10 to 12 minutes, or until golden; cool. Cut into bars.

Makes about 2 dozen.

4 c. quick-cooking oats, uncooked
1 c. brown sugar, packed
3/4 c. butter, melted
1/2 c. honey
1/2 c. sweetened flaked coconut
1/2 c. semi-sweet chocolate chips
1/2 c. chopped nuts
1 t. vanilla extract
1 t. cinnamon
1 t. salt

FRUITED UPSIDE-DOWN GINGERBREAD CAKE

DENISE WEBB
NEWINGTON, GA

My mother used to make this delicious, old-fashioned dessert in the wintertime. It smells wonderful while baking and tastes so good...it's easy to make, too! It always takes me back to being a little girl at home.

Add melted butter to a 9"x9" baking pan; blend in brown sugar. Spread mixture over bottom of pan. Arrange fruit over top; set aside. Prepare gingerbread mix according to package directions; pour batter over fruit. Bake at 350 degrees for 35 to 40 minutes. Immediately turn pan over on a plate; let stand for one to 2 minutes and remove pan. Garnish as desired.

Serves 9.

1/2 c. butter, melted
1/2 c. brown sugar, packed
15-oz. can fruit cocktail, well drained
15-oz. pkg. gingerbread cake mix
Garnish: whipped cream or ice cream

GIANT CHOCOLATE CHIP COOKIE

TINA WRIGHT
ATLANTA, GA

My son asks for this giant cookie as his birthday cake. He likes it so much that when his football team won the championship, he asked me to make a special cookie decorated for the celebration. I've even given it as a gift, tucked into a new pizza box from a nearby pizza shop.

In a large bowl, with an electric mixer on medium speed, beat together butter, sugars and vanilla until light and fluffy. Add eggs, one at a time, beating well. Gradually add flour, baking soda and salt, beating until well blended. Stir in chocolate chips and nuts. Spread dough in a greased 14" round pizza pan. Bake at 375 degrees for 20 to 25 minutes. Set pan on a wire rack to cool. Decorate as desired; cut into wedges or squares to serve.

Makes 16 servings.

1 c. butter, softened
3/4 c. brown sugar, packed
3/4 c. sugar
1 t. vanilla extract
2 eggs
2-1/4 c. all-purpose flour
1 t. baking soda
1 t. salt
2 c. semi-sweet chocolate chips
1 c. chopped walnuts
Optional: frosting, candy sprinkles

Georgia

DEBBY'S ORANGE SHERBET CAKE

DEBBY CONAWAY
ROME, GA

My most-requested cake and also my mom's favorite. It's so pretty, people are amazed at the beautiful color on the inside!

Prepare cake mix according to package directions. Add dry gelatin mix; stir well. Spread batter in 3 greased and floured 9" round cake pans. Bake at 350 degrees until golden, 33 to 36 minutes. Cool completely. For frosting, combine powdered sugar, thawed coconut, sour cream, vanilla and enough orange juice to make a frosting consistency. Set aside one cup frosting. With a serrated knife, halve each layer horizontally. Spread remaining frosting between layers; do not frost top of cake. Combine reserved frosting and whipped topping. Spread over top and sides of cake; sprinkle with canned coconut.

Makes 18 servings.

18-1/4 oz. pkg. orange supreme cake mix

6-oz. pkg. orange gelatin mix

16-oz. pkg. powdered sugar

2 6-oz. pkgs. frozen flaked coconut, thawed

8-oz. container sour cream

1 t. vanilla extract

2 T. frozen orange juice concentrate

12-oz. container frozen whipped topping, thawed

Garnish: 3-1/2 oz. can flaked coconut

PRESENTATION

For a decadent way to serve ice cream, dip the edges of waffle cone bowls into melted white or dark chocolate and then dip them into chopped peanuts, sprinkles or both! Allow the chocolate to setup before stacking them or serving with ice cream.

INDOOR S'MORES

JULIE WARREN
VALDOSTA, GA

My daughter loves s'mores, but we live inside the city limits and can't have a bonfire. This is a great alternative!

3.9-oz. pkg. instant
 chocolate pudding mix
2 T. butter, melted
1 c. mini marshmallows
2 c. cold milk
1 sleeve honey graham
 crackers, finely
 crushed

In a large bowl, whisk together pudding mix and milk for 2 minutes; set aside. In another bowl, mix crushed graham crackers with melted butter. Put 2 heaping tablespoonfuls of cracker mixture into each of 4 to 5 heat-proof small dessert bowls. Add 2 to 3 heaping tablespoonfuls pudding to each bowl. Sprinkle some of remaining cracker mixture over pudding. Refrigerate until pudding is set. Top each bowl with several mini marshmallows. Place under oven broiler for a few seconds, until marshmallows start to turn lightly golden. Watch closely as this happens quickly.

Serves 4 to 5.

CHOCOLATE VELVET PIE

TINA WRIGHT
ATLANTA, GA

This pie is irresistible! My Aunt Betty always brought it to family gatherings...we loved it.

9-inch frozen pie crust,
 unbaked
2 1-oz. sqs. unsweetened
 baking chocolate
14-oz. can sweetened
 condensed milk
2 eggs, well beaten
1 c. water
2 t. vanilla extract
Garnish: whipped cream
Optional: chocolate curls

Bake pie crust according to package directions; set aside. Meanwhile, in a heavy saucepan over medium heat, melt chocolate with condensed milk; stir well and remove from heat. Stir in eggs; stir in water and vanilla. Pour into warm crust. Bake at 400 degrees for 10 minutes. Reduce oven temperature to 300 degrees; bake another 20 minutes, or until center is set. Cool; cover and chill thoroughly. Cut into wedges. Garnish with a dollop of whipped cream and chocolate curls, if desired.

Makes 8 servings.

APPLE BUTTER COOKIES

DEANNE CORONA
HAMPTON, GA

Every September, I like to go to the mountains to get Winesap apples. I love to make apple butter with them. It makes my kitchen smell really nice and apple-y. I make so much apple butter that I decided to do something else with my apple butter...I bake cookies. They freeze really nicely.

Add shortening to a large bowl; work shortening with the back of a spoon until fluffy and creamy. Gradually add brown sugar; mix until light. Stir in egg. In another bowl, sift together flour, baking soda and salt. Add flour mixture to shortening mixture alternately with buttermilk; mix well. Cover and chill until dough is easy to handle. Turn out dough onto a lightly floured surface. Roll out 1/8-inch thick. Cut out cookies with a 2-1/2" round cookie cutter. Sandwich cookies together in pairs, with one teaspoon apple butter in between. Press edges together with a fork. Sprinkle with sugar, if desired. Place cookies on greased baking sheets, one inch apart. Bake at 400 degrees for 12 to 15 minutes.

1/2 c. shortening
1 c. brown sugar, packed
1 egg, beaten
3 c. all-purpose flour
1/2 t. baking soda
1/2 t. salt
1/2 c. buttermilk
1/2 c. apple butter
Optional: sugar

Makes 2 dozen.

JUST FOR FUN

Helen, a small town located about 85 miles north of Atlanta, is a very popular tourist destination. Helen is the third most-visited city in Georgia due to it being a replica of a small Bavarian village nestled in the Blue Ridge Mountains.

SUMMER BLUEBERRY BUCKLE

KATHY COURINGTON
CANTON, GA

We have a farm nearby where we can go to pick blueberries every summer. I love blueberries and like to make this recipe. Good for our ladies' brunches and luncheons...they love it.

1/4 c. butter, softened
3/4 c. sugar
1 egg, beaten
2 c. all-purpose flour
2 t. baking powder
1/2 t. salt
1/2 c. milk
2 c. fresh or frozen
   blueberries, thawed

TOPPING
1/4 c. butter, softened
1/3 c. all-purpose flour
1/2 c. sugar
1/2 t. cinnamon

In a bowl, blend butter and sugar; add egg and beat well. In a separate bowl, sift together flour, baking powder and salt. Stir milk into butter mixture alternately with flour mixture. Gently fold in blueberries; spread batter evenly in a buttered 9"x9" baking pan. Sprinkle with Topping. Bake at 350 degrees for 35 to 40 minutes.

Topping:
Blend all ingredients together.

Makes 4 to 6 servings.

PRESENTATION

For an easy chocolate ganache, microwave equal parts heavy whipping cream and semi-sweet chocolate chips in 15-second increments, until melted, stirring in between.

LIGHT-AS-A-CLOUD CHEESECAKE

DENISE WEBB
NEWINGTON, GA

This is the cake my mom always made when I was growing up. It is delicious and light, especially topped with strawberry syrup or fresh raspberries.

Make Graham Cracker Crust; set aside. Dissolve gelatin mix in boiling water; let stand to room temperature, until set. Meanwhile, in a separate bowl, beat cream cheese until softened. Beat in sugar and vanilla; set aside. Pour chilled milk into another bowl; beat with an electric mixer on medium-high speed until soft peaks form. Fold gelatin mixture into whipped milk. Add to cream cheese mixture; mix gently. Spoon into graham cracker crust; cover and chill.

Graham Cracker Crust:
Combine graham cracker crumbs, sugar and butter. Press into a 13"x9" baking pan; chill.

Makes 15 to 20 servings.

3-oz. pkg. lemon gelatin mix
1 c. boiling water
8-oz. pkg. cream cheese, softened
1 c. sugar
1 t. vanilla extract
12-oz. can evaporated milk, chilled

GRAHAM CRACKER CRUST
2 sleeves graham crackers
1/2 c. sugar crushed
3/4 c. butter, softened

PEACH UPSIDE-DOWN CAKE

TINA WRIGHT
ATLANTA, GA

My Aunt Lillie was well-known for her wonderful pies and cakes. When she brought this wonderful cake to a family picnic, we were in seventh heaven! If you don't have a cast-iron skillet, just use a round cake pan.

1/4 c. plus 1/3 c. butter, divided
1 c. light brown sugar, packed
29-oz. can sliced cling peaches, well drained
4 maraschino cherries, sliced
1/4 c. toasted sliced almonds
2/3 c. sugar
2 eggs, beaten
1-1/2 c. all-purpose flour
1 T. baking powder
1/4 t. salt
1-1/2 t. ground ginger
2/3 c. milk
Garnish: whipped cream

In a 9" cast-iron skillet over medium heat, melt 1/4 cup butter with brown sugar. Cook and stir until sugar is dissolved. Remove from heat. Arrange 3 peach slices in the center of skillet, forming a circle. Arrange remaining slices in a sunburst effect. Scatter sliced cherries and almonds around peach slices; set aside. In a large bowl, blend sugar and remaining butter; beat in eggs. In a separate bowl, combine flour, baking powder, salt and ginger; stir well. Add flour mixture to sugar mixture alternately with milk; mix well. Gently pour batter into skillet over peaches. Bake at 350 degrees for 35 to 40 minutes, until a toothpick inserted in the center tests clean. Immediately invert a serving plate over skillet; turn skillet upside-down over plate. Leave skillet over cake for a few minutes; turn out cake. Serve warm with whipped cream.

Makes 8 servings.

KITCHEN TIP

For a scrumptious dessert in a jiffy, make an ice cream pie! Soften two pints of your favorite ice cream and spread in a graham cracker crust, then freeze. Garnish with whipped topping and cookie crumbs or fresh berries.

PEACH PUFF COBBLER

PENNY SHERMAN
COLUMBUS, GA

My aunt always served this simple dessert when we visited her home in the country. It's delicious warm, topped with ice cream, as well as cold, topped with whipped cream.

Combine reserved syrup, brown sugar and lemon juice in a saucepan. Bring to a boil over medium-high heat; stir until brown sugar is dissolved. Add peaches; remove from heat. In a bowl, stir together biscuit mix, milk and sugar until dough forms. Spread dough in a greased 8"x8" baking pan. Pour hot peach mixture over dough; dot with butter. Sprinkle with cinnamon-sugar. Bake at 450 degrees for 15 to 20 minutes. Serve warm or cold.

Serves 6 to 8.

29-oz. can sliced
   peaches, drained and
   1/2 c. syrup reserved
1/2 c. brown sugar,
   packed
2 t. lemon juice
1 c. biscuit baking mix
1/3 c. evaporated milk
2 T. sugar
2 t. butter, diced
Garnish: cinnamon-
   sugar

MOM'S DATE-NUT CHEWS

BETTY KOZLOWSKI
NEWNAN, GA

Mom baked dozens & dozens of cookies every year at Christmastime to share with friends. These cookies were one of my favorites.

In a large bowl, sift together flour, baking powder, salt and brown sugar. Stir in dates and nuts. Beat eggs and vanilla in a small bowl; blend into flour mixture. Pour batter into a greased 8"x8" baking pan. Bake at 350 degrees for 35 minutes. While still warm, cut into one-inch squares; roll into balls. Roll in powdered sugar, coating well.

Makes 4 dozen.

2/3 c. all-purpose flour
3/4 t. baking powder
1/2 t. salt
1 c. brown sugar, packed
1 c. chopped dates
1 c. chopped nuts
2 eggs
1 t. vanilla extract
Garnish: powdered
   sugar

INDEX

INDEX continued

U.S. to METRIC RECIPE EQUIVALENTS

Volume Measurements

¼ teaspoon. . . . . 1 mL
½ teaspoon. 2 mL
1 teaspoon . . . . 5 mL
1 tablespoon = 3 teaspoons. . . . . . 15 mL
2 tablespoons = 1 fluid ounce . . . . 30 mL
¼ cup. . . . . 60 mL
⅓ cup. . . . . 75 mL
½ cup = 4 fluid ounces. . . . . 125 mL
1 cup = 8 fluid ounces . . . . 250 mL
2 cups = 1 pint = 16 fluid ounces 500 mL
4 cups = 1 quart . . . . 1 L

Weights

1 ounce . . . . 30 g
4 ounces . . . . 120 g
8 ounces . . . . 225 g
16 ounces = 1 pound . . . . 450 g

Baking Pan Sizes
Square
8x8x2 inches . . . . 2 L = 20x20x5 cm
9x9x2 inches . . . . . . 2.5 L = 23x23x5 cm

Rectangular
13x9x2 inches . . . . . 3.5 L = 33x23x5 cm

Loaf
9x5x3 inches . . . . 2 L = 23x13x7 cm

Round
x1½ inches . . . . 1.2 L = 20x4 cm
x1½ inches . . . . 1.5 L = 23x4 cm

Recipe Abbreviations
t. = teaspoon. . . . . ltr. = liter
T. = tablespoon. . . . . oz. = ounce
c. = cup. . . . . lb. = pound
pt. = pint. . . . . .doz. = dozen
qt. = quart. . . . . .pkg. = package
gal. = gallon. . . . . env. = envelope

Oven Temperatures
300° F. . . . . .150° C
325° F. . . . . .160° C
350° F. . . . . .180° C
375° F. . . . . .190° C
400° F. . . . . .200° C
450° F. . . . . .230° C

Kitchen Measurements
A pinch = ⅛ tablespoon
1 fluid ounce = 2 tablespoons
3 teaspoons = 1 tablespoon
4 fluid ounces = ½ cup
2 tablespoons = ⅛ cup
8 fluid ounces = 1 cup
4 tablespoons = ¼ cup
16 fluid ounces = 1 pint
8 tablespoons = ½ cup
32 fluid ounces = 1 quart
16 tablespoons = 1 cup
16 ounces net weight = 1 pound
2 cups = 1 pint
4 cups = 1 quart
4 quarts = 1 gallon

Send us your favorite recipe

and the memory that makes it special for you!*

If we select your recipe for a brand-new **Gooseberry Patch** cookbook, your name will appear right along with it...and you'll receive a FREE copy of the book!

Submit your recipe on our website at

www.gooseberrypatch.com/sharearecipe

*Please include the number of servings and all other necessary information.

Have a taste for more?

Visit www.gooseberrypatch.com to join our Circle of Friends!

• Free recipes, tips and ideas plus a complete cookbook index
• Get mouthwatering recipes and special email offers delivered to your inbox.

You'll also love these cookbooks from **Gooseberry Patch**!

Our Best 5-Ingredient Fresh Family Recipes
A Year of Holidays
Autumn in a Jiffy
Christmas Comfort Foods
Classic Church Potlucks
Our Best Fast, Easy & Delicious Recipes
Grandma's Favorites
Made from Scratch
Mom's Best Sunday Suppers
Our Best Recipes for Cast-Iron Cooking

www.gooseberrypatch.com